# SpringerBriefs in Finance

SpringerBriefs present concise summaries of cutting-edge research and practical applications across a wide spectrum of fields. Featuring compact volumes of 50 to 125 pages, the series covers a range of content from professional to academic. Typical topics might include: a timely report of state-of-the art analytical techniques, a bridge between new research results, as published in journal articles, and a contextual literature review, a snapshot of a hot or emerging topic, an in-depth case study or clinical example, and a presentation of core concepts that students must understand in order to make independent contributions. SpringerBriefs in Finance showcase emerging theory, empirical research, and practical application in corporate finance, banking, financial management, behavioral finance, financial markets, social and entrepreneurial finance, microfinance, and related fields, from a global author community. Briefs are characterized by fast, global electronic dissemination, standard publishing contracts, standardized manuscript preparation and formatting guidelines, and expedited production schedules.

Anna Maria Moisello • Pietro Gottardo

# Risk and Sustainability in Family Businesses

## Exploring ESG Pressures, Organizational Behaviors, and Strategic Responses

Springer

Anna Maria Moisello
Department of Economics and Management
University of Pavia
Pavia, Italy

Pietro Gottardo
Department of Economics and Management
University of Pavia
Pavia, Italy

ISSN 2193-1720 ISSN 2193-1739 (electronic)
SpringerBriefs in Finance
ISBN 978-3-032-19994-2 ISBN 978-3-032-19995-9 (eBook)
https://doi.org/10.1007/978-3-032-19995-9



This Springer imprint is published by the registered company Springer Nature Switzerland AG
The registered company address is: Gewerbestrasse 11, 6330 Cham, Switzerland

# Contents

# Chapter 1
# Introduction

**Abstract** Family businesses are a crucial component of the global economy; however, the issue of risk in these contexts has been addressed in a fragmented manner so far. The literature has gradually recognized the multidimensional nature of risk in family firms, moving beyond purely economic and financial approaches to encompass identity, emotional, and reputational dimensions. However, there remains a lack of theoretical and quantitative systematization that conceptually organizes the concept's multiple meanings and fields of application. At the same time, one of the main emerging areas of risk—that related to ESG controversies—has been little explored in the literature on family businesses, despite its growing relevance for long-term survival and legitimacy. This volume addresses these two gaps through two research questions: RQ1, how risk has been conceptualized and thematized in the literature on family businesses, and what theoretical trajectories and knowledge gaps characterize the field; RQ2, how governance characteristics influence family businesses' exposure to ESG controversy risk. The chapter concludes by presenting the book's structure and providing a summary of the chapters.

**Keywords** Family businesses · Multidimensional risk · Socioemotional wealth · ESG controversies · Governance · Research questions

## 1.1 Introduction

Family businesses are the most widespread and influential form of enterprise in the global economy. According to recent estimates, they account for 70% of global GDP and employ 60% of the worldwide workforce. The top 500 family businesses generate an aggregate turnover of $8.8 trillion and employ 25.1 million people.[1] In the United States, this segment accounts for approximately 54–64% of private GDP

[1] https://www.ey.com/en_gl/insights/family-enterprise/family-business-index accessed on 5th June 2025.



A. M. Moisello, P. Gottardo, *Risk and Sustainability in Family Businesses*, SpringerBriefs in Finance, https://doi.org/10.1007/978-3-032-19995-9_1

and employs 59–62% of the workforce.[2] In Europe, family businesses account for approximately 50% of the GDP and use between 40% and 50% of the private sector workforce.[3]

This phenomenon affects not only micro firms and SMEs but also larger companies, underscoring the importance of the family as an economic and social driver.

The international economic reality has already provided numerous examples of how crises affecting family-owned businesses can have a knock-on effect far beyond the boundaries of the company itself: from the collapse of Parmalat, which shook the entire European financial system with a €14 billion accounting fraud, to the collapse of Lehman Brothers, which triggered the global financial crisis,[4] to the "Indian Enron," Satyam, overwhelmed by a billion-dollar accounting fraud that required direct government intervention to save confidence and jobs.[5] Incidents such as the collapse of Adelphia Communications in the United States (Kidwell, 2017) or the Hanbo case in Korea, which contributed to the Asian financial crisis of 1997 (Quah, 2011), highlight the systemic implications that particular internal dynamics can produce.

Despite its centrality, academic attention has often overlooked the complexity of the risk issue in family businesses (Kempers et al., 2018). Initial studies focused exclusively on economic and financial models when examining risk appetite, comparing family and non-family firms (Anderson & Reeb, 2003). However, it has only recently emerged that risk in these contexts is inherently multidimensional, encompassing not only elements of volatility or asset vulnerability, but also reputational, relational, and identity aspects related to socioemotionalwealth (SEW) (Gomez-Mejia et al., 2007). More recently, the literature has begun to recognize the multifaceted nature of risk in family businesses, emphasizing that the emotional heritage associated with continuity, family identity, reputation, and relationships plays a crucial role in shaping these businesses' strategic choices and risk profiles (Berrone et al., 2012). Theoretical and systematic studies emphasize that risk cannot be interpreted solely in economic and financial terms, but must also encompass reputational, identity, and relational dimensions (Rodrigues et al., 2025). The desire to safeguard this socioemotionalcapital can lead to highly selective perceptions and risk management, sometimes marked by caution, and occasionally by willingness to make risky choices to protect family identity (Ng et al., 2022; Yadav, 2022). Furthermore, generational dynamics and succession processes further complicate the relationship between risk and family businesses, revealing how deeply rooted it is in values and emotions rather than purely economic factors (Ferrari, 2023).

[2] https://www.businessinitiative.org/statistics/small-businesses/family-owned; https://www.familybusinesscenter.com/resources/family-business-facts; https://familybusiness.org/content/measuring-the-financial-impact-of-family-businesses-on-the-US-ec accessed on 5th June 2025.

[3] https://wealthmanagement.bnpparibas/en/insights/news/new-report-family-governance-europe-trends-insights.html accessed on 5th June 2025.

[4] https://www.econcrises.org/2016/11/29/parmalat accessed on 5th June 2025.

[5] https://knowledge.wharton.upenn.edu/article/scandal-at-satyam-truth-lies-and-corporate-governance accessed on 5th June 2025.

A few reviews have sought to systematize this topic (Kempers et al., 2018; Hiebl, 2012; Mismetti et al., 2024), offering useful frameworks and classifications. Nonetheless, the literature still lacks an extensive and integrated treatment of the diverse meanings and implications of risk in family firms, particularly concerning newer challenges such as ESG exposure, reputational legitimacy, and their interactions with governance structures.

Although the literature on risk in family businesses has made significant contributions in historical and theoretical terms (Colli, 2013), it still lacks a comprehensive, systematic, and quantitatively based framework for its conceptual articulations, leaving a considerable knowledge gap about the evolution of new forms of risk, particularly those related to ESG issues.

Our research revolves around two fundamental questions. The first aims to explore how risk has been conceptualized and addressed in the literature on family businesses:

RQ1: *How has risk been conceptualized, addressed, and discussed in the literature on family businesses, and what theoretical dimensions and thematic strands define the field and its knowledge gaps today?*

The second question arises from the observation that although various aspects of risk have been explored, ESG risk—that is, potential exposure to environmental, social, or governance controversies—is under-explored in the literature on family businesses. We know that ESG adoption is often seen by family businesses not only as a regulatory obligation, but as a lever to reduce reputational and strategic risk (Hughes et al., 2025). In fact, there is evidence of a positive correlation between ESG performance and reduced default risk (Liu & Zhang, 2024), but we do not know the determinants of ESG risk in family businesses, and the following question is particularly relevant:

RQ2: *How does the governance of family businesses affect exposure to ESG controversy risk?*

Throughout the volume, the term "risk" is used in a broad, multidimensional sense, encompassing both conditions of exposure to different types of risk (financial, strategic, reputational, ESG) and how such exposure is perceived and managed within family firms. Our study addresses these research questions by adopting a two-pronged approach. Starting from an extensive bibliometric analysis of a corpus of 756 peer-reviewed articles indexed by Scopus and Web of Science, it semantically maps the literature, identifying seven thematic clusters: ownership structure, board structure, and risk; governance, risk, and performance; entrepreneurship, innovation, and risk; internationalization and risk; risk management, reputation, and CSR; emotional dimension and risk; exogenous crises and resilience. It develops the themes of the different clusters, drawing on the literature, and discusses their implications. On the one hand, the analysis highlights areas that require development, for which the bibliometric analysis does not yet reveal a cluster, that is, ESG risk. On the other hand, it offers ideas for development related to the themes that characterize the emerging clusters.

This study concludes by offering an original empirical contribution dedicated to the link between governance structure and exposure to ESG litigation risk. It empirically analyzes how ownership and board characteristics influence the likelihood of being involved in environmental, social, or governance litigation.

Overall, the volume offers three main contributions to the scientific literature.

Firstly, it provides a systematic, multidimensional mapping of the literature on risk in family businesses, thereby overcoming traditional dichotomous classifications between family and non-family businesses. Secondly, it complements prior reviews by expanding the analytical scope and offering a more up-to-date, thematically articulated interpretation of the literature, capable of highlighting the interconnections among areas such as governance, innovation, internationalization, reputation, affectivity, CSR, and systemic crises. Thirdly, it provides an unprecedented empirical contribution to a relatively underexplored yet highly strategic area by examining the relationship between family governance structure and ESG risk.

This work is intended for the academic community, policymakers, and business professionals. For the former, it provides a solid analytical basis for developing new theoretical and empirical lines of inquiry; for the latter, it offers valuable insights into understanding the vulnerabilities and potential of family businesses in a context where risk is no longer just an economic variable but a matter of legitimacy, sustainability, and long-term survival.

## 1.2 Summary and Chapter Breakdown

The book is divided into ten chapters:

**This Chapter: Introduction**

The introductory chapter opens the volume by outlining the context in which the analysis takes place. The chapter highlights how the concept of risk in family firms has evolved from a purely economic and financial perspective to a broader, multifaceted understanding that encompasses socio-emotional, identity, and reputational dimensions. Throughout the volume, risk is understood in a broad sense, referring both to firms' exposure to various types of risk and to how such exposure is perceived and managed within family businesses. However, despite this evolution, a lack of systematization in research on the subject remains, which can hinder the organic reflection of the phenomenon's complexity.

In addition, emphasis is placed on an emerging, previously underinvestigated area of risk in family businesses: ESG (environmental, social, and governance) controversies. The growing salience of such controversies poses new challenges to the legitimacy and sustainability of family firms, particularly given their structural and value-based distinctiveness.

The chapter then explains the two main research questions that guide the entire volume. The first aims to reconstruct how risk is conceptualized in the literature on family businesses, highlighting gaps and prospects for future research. The second aims to investigate how the characteristics of family governance influence companies' exposure to ESG controversy risk.

Finally, the introduction concludes with a detailed presentation of the book's structure, offering a map of the subsequent chapters.

**Chapter 2: Bibliometric Analysis of the Literature on Risk in Family Businesses**

The second chapter outlines the methodological framework underlying the bibliometric survey, which aims to provide a conceptual map of scientific output on the topic of risk in family businesses. Based on an analysis of 756 peer-reviewed articles indexed in the Scopus and Web of Science databases, a semantic network is constructed, organized into seven thematic clusters, with central nodes representing the core research topics. These clusters are: "Governance, risk and performance" (orange cluster), "Ownership structure, board structure and risk" (blue cluster), "Entrepreneurship, innovation, digitalization and risk" (yellow cluster), "Internationalization and global risk" (red cluster), "Risk Management, Reputation, and CSR in Family Businesses" (green cluster), "Emotional dimensions and risk" (purple cluster), and the secondary presenting other risks in family firms: "Exogenous crises and pandemic resilience" (orange/blue cluster). Collectively, they cover themes such as governance, ownership structure, entrepreneurship, internationalization, reputational risk management, ESG, the affective dimension, and responses to exogenous crises.

A significant absence is also highlighted regarding ESG risks, which does not appear a recurring central keyword, despite the growing attention to environmental, social, and governance issues. Even corporate social responsibility, although present within the green cluster, emerges only marginally and is connected to secondary nodes, further underscoring the semantic and conceptual gap in this area.

**Chapter 3: Theories Used in Studies on Risk in Family Businesses**

The third chapter examines the primary theoretical frameworks employed to analyze risk in family businesses. First, Agency Theory stands out as the dominant paradigm, offering analytical tools that help explain conflicts between ownership and control, as well as the implications of family ownership concentration for opacity, opportunism, and strategic conservatism. However, the theory is enriched by two complementary perspectives: Behavioral Agency Theory, which introduces the notion of SEW as a perceptual reference in risk assessment, and the Socioemotional Wealth perspective, which extends the concept of risk to the emotional assets that the family derives from the business: identity, reputation, continuity, and family control.

Completing the picture is Stewardship Theory, which outlines a fiduciary view of family governance grounded in intergenerational responsibility and alignment between business strategy and family values. The chapter then introduces the Resource-Based View and the related notion of familiness, which reinterpret risk-taking as an investment in, or protection of, the idiosyncratic bundle of resources generated by the family–firm nexus, shaping financial, innovative, and succession choices. Finally, Legitimacy Theory shifts the focus to the need to preserve social approval and the "license to operate," showing how disclosure, CSR, and governance decisions are also used strategically to manage perceived risk in the eyes of external stakeholders.

**Chapter 4: Governance, Ownership Structure, and Risk Management in Family Businesses**

The fourth chapter examines the role of governance in risk management in family businesses, integrating two thematic perspectives. On the one hand, in line with the cluster "ownership structure, board structure, and risk" (blue cluster), we analyze the structural characteristics of governance—ownership configuration, board structure, and information transparency—that influence the firm's ability to perceive and manage risk. Concentrated ownership structures, overlap between ownership and control, and poor disclosure can increase exposure to opaque or conservative behavior, limiting competitiveness.

On the other hand, in line with the "governance, risk, and performance" (orange) cluster, the chapter shows how the family nature of governance can foster a more cautious risk appetite oriented toward protecting socioemotionalwealth. However, in the absence of adequate professionalization and transparency on the board, such prudence can become strategic rigidity. Governance thus emerges as a crucial lever for balancing family values and adaptive capacity, thereby determining the risk profile and long-term performance.

**Chapter 5: Innovation, Digitalization, and Risk**

The fifth chapter examines the "entrepreneurship, innovation, digitalization, and risk" cluster (yellow), highlighting how family businesses mitigate risk in these areas given their unique structural and value characteristics. It shows how the adoption of innovative strategies is often conditioned by the tension between the desire to preserve identity and the need for competitive adaptation. Family businesses typically favor incremental forms of innovation and cautious approaches; however, the presence of new generations, external human capital, and more open governance practices can trigger transformation processes in which innovation serves as a tool for both risk mitigation and growth.

**Chapter 6: Internationalization and Global Risk**

The sixth chapter analyzes the relationship between internationalization and risk in family businesses, referring to the "Internationalization and global risk" cluster (red). It examines how family businesses manage risk in their cross-border expansion, focusing on market entry, currency risk management, and exposure to institutional and competitive risks associated with global dimensions. The emotional and identity-based logic that characterizes them often leads to cautious international strategies, grounded in gradual entry and strict selectivity in partners and markets. However, even in this area, generational transition, the adoption of advanced risk management tools, and openness to external expertise appear to be crucial for overcoming cultural rigidity and building resilience.

**Chapter 7: Socioemotional Wealth, Reputation, and CSR in Risk Management**

The seventh chapter analyzes risk management in family businesses through the interaction between the affective dimension, reputation, and social responsibility. Within the "emotional dimension and risk" cluster (purple), the focus is on how affective bonds, identity values, and non-economic goals shape perceptions of risk and responses to uncertainty. SEW is an ambivalent asset: on the one hand, it promotes cohesion and resilience; on the other, it can generate decision-making rigidity, particularly at critical moments such as generational succession, where risk is filtered through complex emotional dynamics.

At the same time, with respect to the "reputation, CSR, and risk" cluster (green), the chapter demonstrates that social responsibility is often adopted as a strategic response to stakeholder pressure and as a tool to strengthen legitimacy. Reputation plays a central role in risk management, acting as both a symbolic shield and a potential vulnerability factor if inconsistencies arise between stated values and actual practices. CSR is effective only when authentically integrated into the company's identity, thereby contributing to organizational resilience and reducing uncertainty in contexts of high reputational exposure.

**Chapter 8: Family Governance and ESG Controversy Risk: An Empirical Analysis**

Addressing an underexplored issue, the eighth chapter adopts a comparative approach to examining the exposure of family and non-family businesses to ESG controversies, defined as adverse events in the environmental, social, or governance spheres. The chapter presents an empirical analysis based on a panel of 3820 observations from a sample of European listed companies between 2013 and 2022, utilizing OLS and 2SLS regression models. The results highlight how governance variables influence the incidence of ESG controversies differently in the two types of companies. In family firms, a higher share of family ownership is associated with a lower probability of controversies, while cultural diversity on the board can increase the risk. The size of the board of directors and the company's profitability further modulate this exposure. The chapter critically discusses these findings in light of Socioemotional Wealth and Legitimacy theories, highlighting the conditions under which family governance can serve as a resource or a source of vulnerability in ESG risk management. The theoretical, managerial, and regulatory implications suggest the need for greater attention to family control configurations, diversity management, and board structuring in family businesses seeking to strengthen their reputational and sustainable resilience.

**Chapter 9: Other Types of Risks in Family Firms**

The ninth chapter analyzes the responses of family businesses to systemic crises, such as the COVID-19 pandemic and the 2008 financial crisis. It develops the thematic "Exogenous crises and pandemic resilience" cluster (orange/blue). The analysis highlights a predominantly reactive resilience model based on internal cohesion, trust capital, and financial prudence, which has enabled short-term containment but has also revealed structural limitations in strategic adaptability.

In the absence of formal Enterprise Risk Management systems, the overlap between family and decision-making logic has sometimes reduced organizational agility, highlighting a vulnerability associated with excessive concentration of power. However, the chapter notes that in some contexts, the shock has triggered transformative dynamics, with intergenerational leadership, forced innovation, and digitalization emerging as signs of an evolution toward more proactive forms of resilience. The crisis is thus seen not only as a stress test for SEW but also as a catalyst for new risk-management trajectories in family firms.

**Chapter 10: Conclusions: Contributions to Literature and Lines of Development for Future Research**

The tenth chapter provides a theoretical summary and critical systematization of the volume, offering a detailed reconstruction of the main findings that emerged in the previous chapters. Starting from the bibliometric and conceptual analysis conducted, the text proposes an original reading of risk in family businesses, structured around five lines of theoretical contribution: the configuration of prevailing interpretative approaches, the reconceptualization of family resilience, the relational and affective nature of risk, the role of governance as a strategic lever, and the connection between entrepreneurship, reputation, and sustainability. These interpretive axes introduce a critical, integrated perspective that enriches the scientific debate on family business.

The chapter concludes by developing an original research agenda that identifies five priority areas for future studies: ownership structures; governance and disclosure; life cycle, succession, and financial structure; innovation and digitalization; and CSR, ESG, and reputational risk management. The aim is to provide the scientific community with a guidance tool that highlights the specific nature of risk in family contexts and promotes multidimensional interpretations that are sensitive to the organizational, institutional, and generational complexity of these businesses.

## References


Anderson, R. C., & Reeb, D. M. (2003). Founding-family ownership and firm performance: Evidence from the S&P 500. *Journal of Finance, 58*(3), 1301–1328.

Berrone, P., Cruz, C., & Gomez-Mejia, L. R. (2012). Socioemotional wealth in family firms: Theoretical dimensions, assessment approaches, and agenda for future research. *Family Business Review, 25*(3), 258–279.

Colli, A. (2013). Family firms between risks and opportunities: A literature review. *Socio-Economic Review, 11*(3), 577–599.

Ferrari, F. (2023). The postponed succession: An investigation of the obstacles hindering business transmission planning in family firms. *Journal of Family Business Management, 13*(2), 412–431.

Gómez-Mejía, L. R., Haynes, K. T., Núñez-Nickel, M., Jacobson, K. J., & Moyano-Fuentes, J. (2007). Socioemotional wealth and business risks in family-controlled firms: Evidence from Spanish olive oil mills. *Administrative Science Quarterly, 52*(1), 106–137.

Hiebl, M. R. (2012). Risk aversion in family firms: What do we really know? *The Journal of Risk Finance, 14*(1), 49–70. "Risk behavior of family firms".

Hughes, M., Hu, Q., Simeonova, B., Ge, B., Issah, W. B., Jack, S., ... & Dai, S. (2025). *ESG in family firms: A review of research, regulations and practice guidance*.

Kempers, M., Leitterstorf, M. P., & Kammerlander, N. (2018). Risk behavior of family firms: A literature review, framework, and research agenda. *The Palgrave handbook of heterogeneity among family firms*, 431-460.

Kidwell, R. E. (2017). Adelphia Communications: The public company that became a private piggy bank: A case of fraud in the Rigas family firm. In *Handbook of frauds, scams, and swindles* (pp. 213–228). Routledge.

Liu, B., & Zhang, X. (2024). The impact of ESG and executive structure on the default risk of family businesses: Evidence from China. *Finance Research Letters, 61*, 104956.

Mismetti, M., Sangermano, A., Del Bosco, B., & Bergamaschi, M. (2024). Understanding the multiple facets of risk in family firms: A review of the literature and a framework for future research. *Journal of Business Research, 183*, 114844.

Ng, P. Y., Dayan, M., & Makri, M. (2022). Influence of socioemotional wealth on non-family managers' risk taking and product innovation in family businesses. *Cross Cultural & Strategic Management, 29*(2), 297–319.

Quah, J. S. (2011). Chapter 9 South Korea. In *Curbing corruption in Asian countries: An impossible dream?* (pp. 307–340). Emerald Group.

Rodrigues, P. P., Pai, P. K., Joshi, H. G., & Prabhu, K. N. (2025). Influence of socioemotional-wealth on entrepreneurial orientation in family firms: A bibliometric analysis and systematic review. *Business Perspectives and Research, 13*(2), 206–225.

Yadav, S. (2022). A socioemotional wealth perspective on innovation in family firms: Review and theoretical extension. *International Journal of Indian Culture and Business Management, 27*(1), 31–50.

# Chapter 2
# Bibliometric Analysis of the Literature on Risk in Family Businesses

**Abstract** This chapter presents the study's methodological design based on a bibliometric analysis of the scientific literature on risk in family businesses. Using the Scopus and Web of Science databases and applying rigorous search strategies, a corpus of 756 peer-reviewed articles published up to March 10, 2025, was constructed. The analysis, conducted using VOSviewer, enabled mapping of semantic co-occurrences and the identification of seven main thematic clusters, which are developed and discussed in the following chapters. The results reveal a fragmented yet growing field of study in which risk management is addressed across the dimensions of governance, innovation, internationalization, CSR, and resilience. The absence of a systematic focus on ESG risk signals a significant knowledge gap, opening new avenues of research. The picture is completed by an analysis of citations, which identifies the most influential contributions in outlining the relationship between family control, risk, and performance.

**Keywords** Bibliometric analysis · Keyword co-occurrence · Thematic clusters · Thematic evolution · Risk

## 2.1 Methodology

The starting point of this study is a bibliometric analysis of the scientific literature on risk in family businesses aimed at identifying the main lines of research and highlighting any unexplored knowledge gaps. In line with established approaches in the methodological literature (Aparicio et al., 2021), the research strategy was defined in advance, including the selection of databases and keywords and the establishment of inclusion and exclusion criteria. Data extraction was conducted on March 10, 2025, by querying the Scopus and Web of Science Core Collection (WoS) databases, which were selected for their recognized multidisciplinary



A. M. Moisello, P. Gottardo, *Risk and Sustainability in Family Businesses*, SpringerBriefs in Finance, https://doi.org/10.1007/978-3-032-19995-9_2

coverage and reliability in identifying peer-reviewed scientific publications (Pranckutė, 2021; AlRyalat et al., 2019). The collection process involved the application of Boolean operators to combine keywords that capture the landscape of articles on risk in family businesses as follows: ("family entrepreneurship" OR "family firm" OR "family business*" OR "family company*" OR "family owned firm*" OR "family owned company*" OR "family-owned business" OR "family-owned enterprise" OR "family-controlled company*" OR "family-controlled firm" OR "family-controlled business" OR "family-controlled enterprise" OR "family enterprise" OR "family-run" OR "family managed business" OR "family owner" OR "family control" OR "family influence" OR "family CEO" OR "family member" OR "family ownership" OR "family involvement" OR "family director" OR "family-owned" OR "family-controlled" OR "family-run" OR "family controlled company*" OR "family-controlled firm" OR "family-controlled business" OR "family-controlled enterprises" OR "family enterprises" OR "family-run businesses" OR "family-run company*" OR "family-run firms" OR "family-run enterprises" OR "family-managed businesses" OR "family owners" OR "family members" OR "family directors" OR "chaebols" OR "family corporation") AND ("risk*"). The selection of products, as detailed in Fig. 2.1, involved an initial screening of papers using strict inclusion and exclusion criteria, removal of duplicates, and manual screening based on relevance criteria. The final sample consists of 756 articles.

The VOSviewer software and Biblioshiny, part of the R package, were used to analyze bibliometric data, which allow the construction and visualization of maps based on bibliometric networks (Van Eck & Waltman, 2010; Aria & Cuccurullo, 2017). A co-occurrence analysis of the authors' keywords was conducted to identify recurring themes and connections among central concepts, thereby outlining the state of the art in scientific knowledge on risk in family businesses in a structured manner. To complement this, a citation analysis was conducted to identify the ten most influential articles defined as those with the highest absolute citation counts. This approach, widely recognized in the literature (Leydesdorff & Bornmann, 2016), allows us to highlight the works that have gained the most academic visibility, although it does have some limitations: the cumulative effect of time, the weight of self-citations, and the influence of editorial prestige can distort the perception of the actual impact on the development of studies in the area (Tahamtan et al., 2016).

## 2.2 Keyword Co-occurrence and Cluster Identification

The bibliometric map provides a visual summary of the main semantic co-occurrences in the literature on risk in family businesses, organizing academic contributions into distinct but interconnected thematic clusters (Fig. 2.2).

The orange cluster—"Governance, risk, and performance"—highlights the link between performance and risk in family businesses, focusing particularly on how

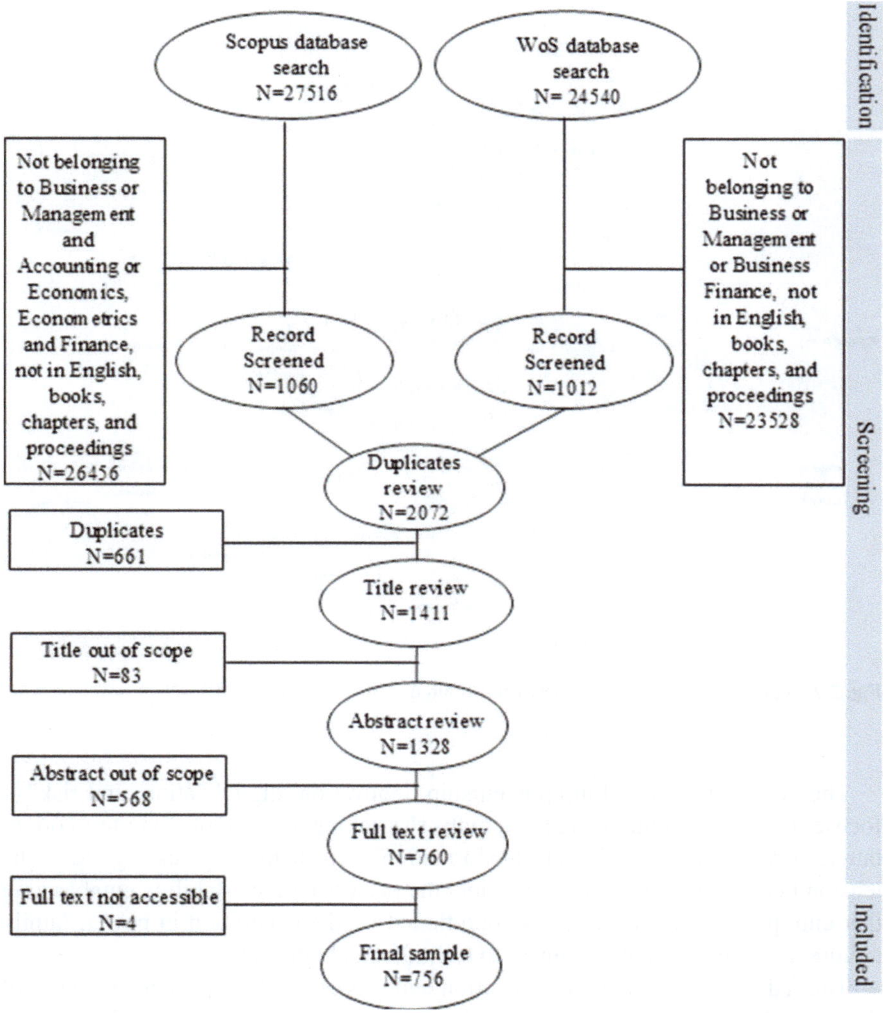


**Fig. 2.1** The article selection process. (Source: Authors' own work)

family ownership, ownership concentration, and risk propensity influence value creation. The cluster includes studies that highlight the role of family governance, information transparency, and agency mechanisms in modulating the relationship between risk and performance.

The blue cluster—"Ownership structure, board structure, and risk"—focuses on ownership structure and control mechanisms. Keywords include corporate governance, ownership structure, family ownership, agency theory, and board of directors. This area analyzes how governance architectures, the role of independent directors, and the presence of family leadership influence risk propensity or aversion in corporate decisions.

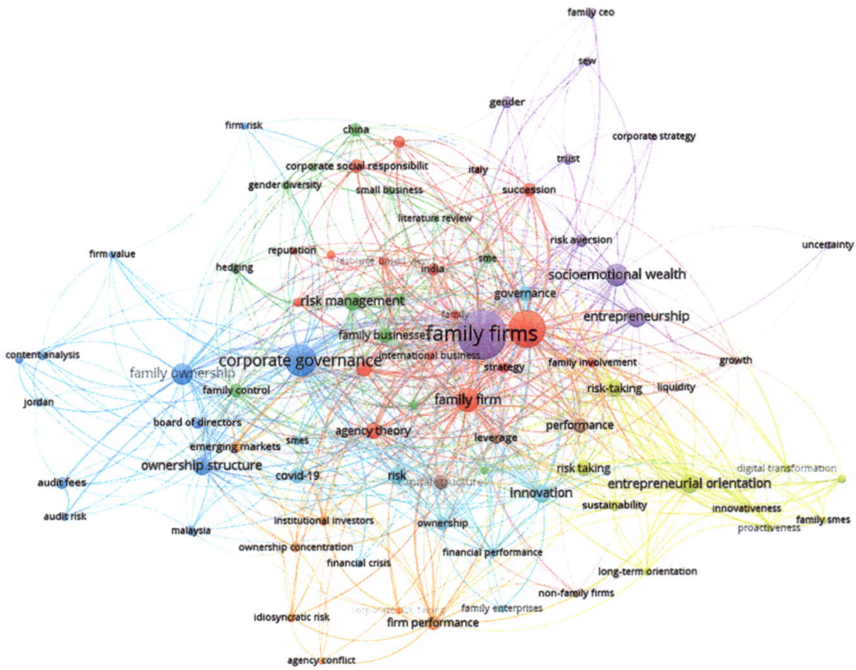


**Fig. 2.2** Keywords co-occurrence network. (Source: Authors' own work)

The yellow cluster—"Entrepreneurship, innovation, digitalization, and risk"—focuses on keywords including proactivity, risk-taking, innovation, long-term orientation, performance, and digital transformation. This thematic block highlights the tension between openness to change and the preservation of stability, emphasizing that entrepreneurial orientation is conditioned by the generation in power, family culture, and the degree of openness to technological renewal.

The red cluster—"Internationalization and global risk"—represents the core of the network and includes keywords such as family firm, strategy, succession, SMEs, and internationalization. This group focuses on the primary strategic choices that family businesses face over time, particularly during generational transitions, growth, and internationalization, in which the family dimension profoundly shapes perceptions and assumptions about risk.

The green cluster—"Risk Management, Reputation, and CSR in Family Businesses"—includes keywords such as risk management, reputation, and resource-based view. Here, the focus shifts to operational strategies and family capabilities as levers for dealing with uncertainty. The relationship between reputational capital and resilience is examined in depth, with particular attention to the role of intangible assets in risk management.

The purple cluster—"Emotional dimension and risk"—revolves around value and psychological concepts. The keywords highlighted are socioemotional wealth, risk aversion, trust, gender, succession, and family involvement. In this cluster, risk is reinterpreted in light of emotional values, the preservation of family identity, and the maintenance of symbolic continuity.

Finally, the map reveals a secondary orange/blue cluster—"Exogenous crises and pandemic resilience"—dedicated to the impact of the COVID-19 pandemic. Although the keyword "COVID" appears blue due to its liminal position between multiple semantic domains, the algorithm places it in a cohesive cluster (orange) that includes concepts such as resilience, crisis, shock, and response strategies. This confirms the cross-cutting and systemic nature of the pandemic crisis in recent literature, as reflected in the analysis of strategic responses adopted by family businesses under stress, with a focus on preserving SEW, accelerating innovation, and absorbing systemic shocks.

A significant observation concerns the absence of the ESG (Environmental, Social, and Governance) theme from the bibliometric map: neither as an autonomous cluster nor as a recurring keyword. Even corporate social responsibility, although present, is marginal and connected to secondary nodes. This absence is all the more significant given the growing salience of the ESG debate and its direct connection to risk management, particularly in the context of family businesses. This semantic gap suggests the need for new systematic studies in this area, aimed at highlighting how the peculiarities of family business governance can affect ESG risk, for example, by influencing the propensity to engage in ESG controversies.

## 2.3 Thematic Evolution

To complete the thematic framework, the analysis was extended to a diachronic perspective by tracing the thematic evolution of keywords. The network was divided into five sub-periods (1995–2010, 2011–2018, 2019–2021, 2022–2024, 2025) to trace connections among recurring themes across time periods. The flow diagram enables us to trace the continuity and discontinuity of the main research trajectories on risk in family businesses, highlighting which conceptual cores consolidate over time, which transform, and which emerge only in more recent phases (Fig. 2.3).

In the first period (1995–2010), the literature appears still embryonic and highly contextualized. The prevailing themes center on the keywords "family business" and "family firm," alongside references to risk assessment and management and to specific country cases, such as China. Risk is primarily addressed in descriptive terms and tied to particular national or sectoral contexts, rather than as an autonomous theoretical construct.

In the second period (2011–2018), the thematic network broadens and becomes more structured. Alongside the continuity of family firms and family businesses, corporate governance, ownership, and capital structure emerge, while entrepreneurship appears as a new focus. During this phase, a progressive shift in focus is observed toward the implications of family control on investment and growth

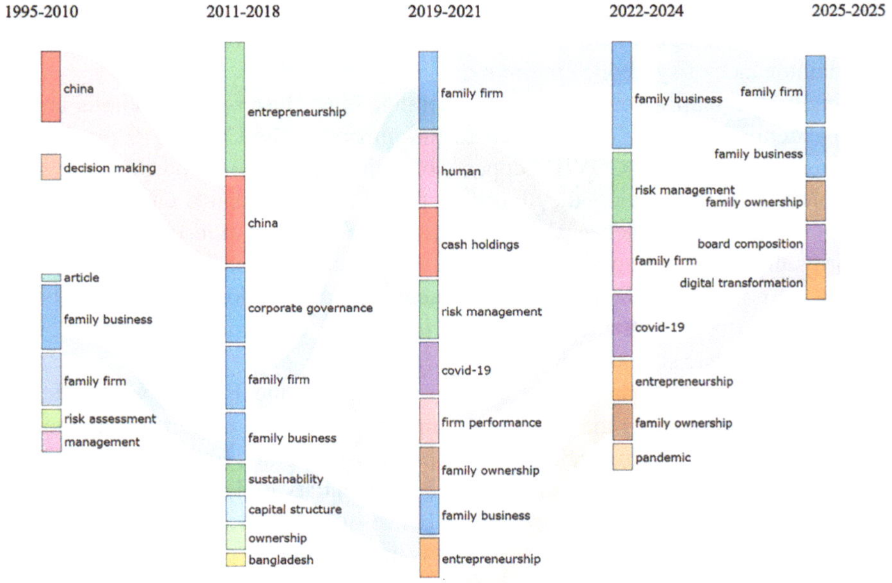


**Fig. 2.3** Thematic evolution. (Source: Authors' own work)

decisions, with the addition of topics such as sustainability and additional geographical references (Bangladesh), which signal greater empirical diversification.

The period 2019–2021 marks an actual turning point. While family firms and family businesses remain central, risk management, family ownership, and firm performance are coming to the forefront, as COVID-19 emerges. Risk is thus being reinterpreted from a more operational and systemic perspective, as, on the one hand, interest in management tools and the consequences for corporate performance grows. On the other, the pandemic introduces an exogenous shock that tests the resilience of family businesses.

These trajectories are consolidating in the 4 years 2022–2024. Risk management and family ownership remain central to family firms and family businesses, while entrepreneurship and the COVID-19 pandemic continue to be key junctures. Recent literature, therefore, tends to combine the analysis of entrepreneurial choices with the study of crisis response strategies, emphasizing the role of family specificities in adaptation processes.

Finally, in the most recent sub-period (2025), thematic evolution highlights the persistence of the family firm/family business/family ownership nucleus and the emergence of issues such as board composition and digital transformation. This suggests a progressive focus on governance body configurations and the challenges posed by digital transformation, interpreted through the lens of risk and the redefinition of control mechanisms.

## 2.4 Content Analysis of the Ten Most Cited Papers

The citation analysis identified the ten most influential articles in the literature on risk in family businesses. These works provide a multidimensional lens for understanding the relationship among family structure, risk-taking, and performance, organized thematically to reflect the main clusters identified in the semantic co-occurrence map.

Some studies fall within the research area exploring the relationship among governance, risk, and performance. This is the case of McConaughy et al. (2001), who show that family-controlled firms have a more conservative capital structure, superior performance, and more prudent management, characterized by low levels of debt. Similarly, Anderson et al. (2009) emphasize the crucial role of information transparency in family businesses, demonstrating that management opacity, while protecting family control, increases perceived risk for investors and external stakeholders.

Closely related are contributions focusing on ownership structure and control mechanisms, such as George et al. (2005), which show that family CEOs and family top management are less inclined to pursue internationalization, highlighting the influence of governance structures and family identity in decision-making processes. Block (2012), focusing on companies founded by individuals, contrasts the decision-making agility and high R&D productivity of these companies with the greater caution and internal conflict that often characterize structured family businesses.

Several contributions examine the relationship among entrepreneurship, innovation, and risk. Zahra (2005) provides a foundational theoretical reference, emphasizing that family ownership can encourage entrepreneurial orientation and a propensity for selective risk, but that the founder's longevity can inhibit openness to innovation. Naldi et al. (2007) analyze Swedish family SMEs and find a lower propensity to take risks than their non-family counterparts, despite a specific capacity for innovation and proactivity. However, the negative relationship between risk and performance that emerges suggests an unresolved tension between entrepreneurial drive and managerial caution. Patel and Chrisman (2014) offer further insights in this regard, illustrating how family businesses adopt a risk-modulation logic, investing in R&D under favorable conditions and favoring incremental and less volatile approaches in stable situations.

A significant part of the literature then focuses on the affective and value dimension of risk, particularly through the concept of socioemotional wealth (SEW). Gómez-Mejía et al. (2007) propose a model in which family businesses, while willing to accept economic risks, avoid strategic decisions that could compromise internal cohesion, family identity, or control. This approach is further supported by Gómez-Mejía et al. (2010), which highlights that strategic diversification is often avoided due to a reluctance to engage with cultural and operational contexts perceived as distant. Lumpkin et al. (2010), also within the SEW perspective, explore the effect of long-term orientation, highlighting how it promotes autonomy and innovation but limits competitive aggressiveness and risk-taking.

Finally, some contributions address the issues of growth and internationalization of family businesses, investigating how the family component influences risk-taking in expansion decisions. In this context, strategies are often conditioned by a logic of continuity, identity, and stability, rather than by pure economic rationality.

Taken together, the ten most cited articles offer a detailed and coherent representation of risk in family businesses, distributed among approaches that focus on governance, ownership structure, the drive for innovation, strategic choices, and value dynamics. Risk-taking emerges from a unique combination of rational, emotional, and cultural factors that reflect the particular nature of family businesses, their constant tension between preservation and change, and the sector's heterogeneity.

Overall, the ten most influential articles are distributed across the main thematic clusters identified by the bibliometric analysis and thus provide the conceptual backbone that guides the discussion developed in the subsequent chapters (Table 2.1).

**Table 2.1** Top ten papers ranked by number of citations

| Author | Aim | Cluster | Theory | TC |
|---|---|---|---|---|
| Gomez-Mejia et al. (2007) | To investigate the relationship between SEW and risks in family-owned businesses within the context of Spanish olive oil mills. | Affective dimension and risk (Purple) | BAM/SEW | 2668 |
| Gomez-Mejia et al. (2010) | To investigate the diversification decisions of family firms compared to non-family firms | Affective dimension and risk (Purple) | Agency theory, SEW, BAM | 1013 |
| Zahra (2005) | To investigate the conditions under which family firms promote entrepreneurial activities | Entrepreneurship, innovation, and risk (Yellow) | Agency theory | 886 |
| Naldi et al. (2007) | To investigate the relationship between risk-taking, entrepreneurship, and performance in family firms | Entrepreneurship, innovation, and risk (Yellow) | Agency theory | 881 |
| Block (2012) | To investigate ownership and management dimensions of family and founder firms regarding R&D intensity and productivity | Ownership structure, board structure, and risk (Blue) | Agency theory | 482 |
| Lumpkin et al. (2010) | To investigate long-term orientation (LTO) as a firm-level phenomenon in family businesses, linking it to entrepreneurial outcomes | Affective dimension and risk (Purple) | Stewardship theory/Agency theory | 462 |
| George et al. (2005) | To investigate how ownership structures of SMEs affect their risk-taking and internationalization efforts | Internationalization and risk (Red) | Agency theory/ RBV | 435 |

(continued)

**Table 2.1** (continued)

| Author | Aim | Cluster | Theory | TC |
|---|---|---|---|---|
| Anderson et al. (2009) | To investigate how founder or heir ownership affects corporate transparency and minority investor risks | Governance, Risk and Performance (Orange) | Agency theory/ Entrenchment hypothesis | 411 |
| Mcconaughy et al. (2001) | To investigate the impact of founding family control on firm performance, capital structure, and value | Governance, Risk and Performance (Orange) | Agency theory | 369 |
| Patel and Chrisman (2014) | To investigate the investment behaviors of family firms' R&D, emphasizing the SEW role in their risk-taking propensities. | Entrepreneurship, innovation, and risk (Yellow) | SEW | 325 |

# References


AlRyalat, S. A. S., Malkawi, L. W., & Momani, S. M. (2019). Comparing bibliometric analysis using PubMed, Scopus, and Web of Science databases. *JoVE (Journal of Visualized Experiments), 152*, e58494.

Anderson, R. C., Duru, A., & Reeb, D. M. (2009). Founders, heirs, and corporate opacity in the United States. *Journal of Financial Economics, 92*(2), 205–222.

Aparicio, G., Ramos, E., Casillas, J. C., & Iturralde, T. (2021). Family business research in the last decade: A bibliometric review. *European Journal of Family Business, 11*(1), 33–43.

Aria, M., & Cuccurullo, C. (2017). bibliometrix: An R-tool for comprehensive science mapping analysis. *Journal of Informetrics, 11*(4), 959–975.

Block, J. H. (2012). R&D investments in family and founder firms: An agency perspective. *Journal of Business Venturing, 27*(2), 248–265.

George, G., Wiklund, J., & Zahra, S. A. (2005). Ownership and the internationalization of small firms. *Journal of Management, 31*(2), 210–233.

Gómez-Mejía, L. R., Haynes, K. T., Núñez-Nickel, M., Jacobson, K. J., & Moyano-Fuentes, J. (2007). Socioemotional wealth and business risks in family-controlled firms: Evidence from Spanish olive oil mills. *Administrative Science Quarterly, 52*(1), 106–137.

Gomez-Mejia, L. R., Makri, M., & Kintana, M. L. (2010). Diversification decisions in family-controlled firms. *Journal of Management Studies, 47*(2), 223–252.

Leydesdorff, L., & Bornmann, L. (2016). The operationalization of "fields" as WoS subject categories (WCs) in evaluative bibliometrics: The cases of "library and information science" and "science & technology studies". *Journal of the Association for Information Science and Technology, 67*(3), 707–714.

Lumpkin, G. T., Brigham, K. H., & Moss, T. W. (2010). Long-term orientation: Implications for the entrepreneurial orientation and performance of family businesses. *Entrepreneurship & Regional Development, 22*(3–4), 241–264.

McConaughy, D. L., Matthews, C. H., & Fialko, A. S. (2001). Founding family controlled firms: Performance, risk, and value. *Journal of Small Business Management, 39*(1), 31–49.

Naldi, L., Nordqvist, M., Sjöberg, K., & Wiklund, J. (2007). Entrepreneurial orientation, risk taking, and performance in family firms. *Family Business Review, 20*(1), 33–47.

Patel, P. C., & Chrisman, J. J. (2014). Risk abatement as a strategy for R&D investments in family firms. *Strategic Management Journal, 35*(4), 617–627.

Pranckutė, R. (2021). Web of Science (WoS) and Scopus: The titans of bibliographic information in today's academic world. *Publications, 9*(1), 12.

Tahamtan, I., Safipour Afshar, A., & Ahamdzadeh, K. (2016). Factors affecting number of citations: A comprehensive review of the literature. *Scientometrics, 107*, 1195–1225.

Van Eck, N., & Waltman, L. (2010). Software survey: VOSviewer, a computer program for bibliometric mapping. *Scientometrics, 84*(2), 523–538.

Zahra, S. A. (2005). Entrepreneurial risk taking in family firms. *Family Business Review, 18*(1), 23–40.

# Chapter 3
# Theories Used in Studies on Risk in Family Businesses

**Abstract** This chapter examines the theories used in the literature on risk in family businesses. Agency Theory is the dominant framework for analyzing conflicts between ownership and control, information risks, and opportunistic practices in family-controlled companies. Behavioral Agency Theory and Socioemotional Wealth Theory, by contrast, explore the affective and identity dimensions that shape risk perception, explaining why families tend to be averse to decisions that threaten continuity or reputation. Stewardship Theory proposes a fiduciary view of family governance, in which strategic caution reflects intergenerational values and moral commitment. The Resource-Based View (RBV) and the related notion of familiness shift the focus to the idiosyncratic bundle of tangible and intangible resources that condition both risk-taking and the capacity to absorb shocks in family firms. Finally, Legitimacy Theory clarifies how risk decisions are influenced by the need to preserve social approval and a "license to operate" within institutional and community contexts, particularly through disclosure, governance, and corporate social responsibility choices. This chapter examines how the main theories have been applied to investigate various aspects of risk in family businesses, which will be explored in the subsequent chapters.

**Keywords** Agency Theory · Behavioral Agency Theory · Socioemotional wealth · Stewardship Theory · Resource-based view · Legitimacy Theory · Risk

## 3.1 Agency Theory

Agency theory is the most widely accepted framework for analyzing risk in family businesses, enabling us to understand the dynamics that arise from the overlap between ownership and control, as well as the implications of family concentration. Agency theory (Meckling & Jensen, 1976) is the primary theoretical framework for understanding how the separation between ownership and control generates information asymmetries and conflicts of interest, which, in turn, influence the quality of decisions and the level of business risk. In family businesses, this theory has been



A. M. Moisello, P. Gottardo, *Risk and Sustainability in Family Businesses*, SpringerBriefs in Finance, https://doi.org/10.1007/978-3-032-19995-9_3

extended to encompass two primary forms of conflict: type I, between managers and shareholders; and type II, between majority shareholders (the family) and minority shareholders. While the former tends to be reduced by the overlap between ownership and management, the latter can intensify due to the risk of expropriation and the family's opportunistic use of power. In the context of governance, it is used to highlight how the presence of dominant family shareholders reduces Type I (manager-shareholder) conflicts but fuels Type II conflicts, generating risks of expropriation and information opacity (Acero & Alcalde, 2016). In context with weak investor protection, as observed by Abid et al. (2018) in Pakistan, family concentration undermines the effectiveness of auditing mechanisms, thereby favoring earnings management. This is also reflected in the quality of risk disclosure, which tends to be lower in family businesses with high ownership concentration, due to entrenchment and the desire to keep sensitive information confidential (Ismail et al., 2014; Al Maani et al., 2025).

In this context, Anderson et al. (2009) integrate the entrenchment hypothesis with agency theory, demonstrating that in family businesses controlled by founders or heirs, information opacity is strategically used to extract private benefits at the expense of minority shareholders, exacerbating type II conflicts.

According to agency theory, the performance of family businesses is interpreted as an unstable balance between efficiency resulting from reduced control costs and inefficiencies due to conservative or opportunistic choices: Baek et al. (2016) show that the presence of family CEOs profoundly changes the trade-offs between risk and return in capital decisions, while Block (2012) highlights that risk aversion, linked to the protection of family capital, can reduce investment in R&D. Similarly, Martinez-Ferrero et al. (2016) emphasize how high ownership concentration can hinder innovation and encourage excessive control, to the detriment of sustainable growth. However, some studies suggest that inclusive governance mechanisms, such as the presence of large shareholders (Boubaker et al., 2016) or independent directors, can mitigate these risks, thereby contributing to corporate resilience.

George (2005) combine agency theory with the resource-based view to explain how risk management and access to distinctive resources in family contexts depend on the degree of family control. Family ownership can influence both strategic decisions and the ability to absorb and leverage critical resources, such as reputation and managerial skills.

Agency theory also provides relevant insights into succession, particularly when combined with other perspectives, such as socioemotional wealth (SEW). Succession involves a potential trade-off between family continuity and economic rationality. Meier and Thelisson (2020) demonstrate that the coexistence of affective and economic logic can exacerbate agency conflicts in decision-making, thereby increasing the risk of strategic conservatism or instability. In this light, Zahra (2005) develops a model in which ownership structure and family involvement influence entrepreneurial risk-taking, suggesting that succession is not just a transition event but a critical node for long-term risk management.

In the field of Corporate Social Responsibility (CSR), agency theory is often combined with signaling theory to explain voluntary disclosure and social responsibility practices as tools for reducing information asymmetry. Alshirah et al. (2020) show that CSR can serve both to reassure investors about risk management and to signal solidity. Yang et al. (2023) integrate agency and SEW theory to demonstrate that family businesses use CSR to protect their socioemotionalwealth, mitigating the risk of share devaluation.

Regarding systemic risk, agency theory helps explain how the presence of family managers or the lack of separation between ownership and control can exacerbate a firm's vulnerabilities in unstable macroeconomic contexts. D'Este and Carabelli (2022) demonstrate that family businesses with strong family involvement in management exhibit greater exposure to systemic risk due to a tendency toward idiosyncratic, poorly diversified decisions. Similarly, Shahzad et al. (2025) apply the concepts of "interest convergence" and "managerial entrenchment" to analyze zero-leverage policy as an adverse response to risk, emphasizing that extreme levels of control can incentivize self-serving behavior, thereby reducing the firm's ability to respond flexibly to market shocks.

Reputation also emerges as a central element in the relationship between agency theory and risk. The protection of socioemotional capital leads families to exercise caution in their strategic choices, especially in contexts of high public visibility. Saghi-Zedek and Tarazi (2015) demonstrate that, while excessive control can lead to opportunistic behavior under normal conditions, during crises, families tend to support firms through "propping up" practices to avoid reputational damage.

Ultimately, agency theory is paramount for understanding the institutional context. Its institutionalized form allows us to understand how legal systems, the quality of public governance, and local culture influence agency costs and risk perception. La Rosa et al. (2020) demonstrate that ownership structure influences the cost of capital through earnings management mechanisms shaped by the legal context, whereas Bodnaruk et al. (2017) highlight that in countries with weak investor protection, the political connections of family businesses can mitigate perceived risk for foreign investors.

### *3.1.1 Behavioral Agency Theory*

*Behavioral Agency Theory* (BAT), formalized by Wiseman and Gomez-Mejia (1998), extends classical Agency Theory by integrating psychological and behavioral elements to explain strategic decisions in contexts characterized by strong emotional and symbolic involvement. According to this theory, agents do not simply maximize economic performance but rather orient their choices toward protecting specific psychological reference points, seeking to avoid perceived losses relative to these reference points. This perspective is particularly well-suited to the analysis of family businesses, where the predominant reference point is socioemotional wealth (SEW), that is, the intangible assets comprising family identity, emotional ties, organizational control, and reputation (Gómez-Mejía et al., 2007).

In the BAT framework, SEW is not simply a cultural preference, but represents a cognitive lens through which risk is perceived, interpreted, and managed. When a strategy even potentially threatens SEW—as in the case of ownership dilution, the entry of external investors, or the loss of the family name in the brand—family businesses tend to reject even profitable opportunities, showing a marked aversion to risk (Gómez-Mejía et al., 2007; Berrone et al., 2012). BAT has been used to analyze decisions such as generational succession, the adoption of innovations, openness to external capital, and the management of reputational crises, revealing how strategic choices are strongly influenced by the centrality of the family as a "perceptual unit" of risk (Alessandri et al., 2018).

## 3.2 Socioemotional Wealth Perspective

The Socioemotional Wealth Theory perspective has established itself as one of the most fruitful and cross-cutting theoretical paradigms for analyzing risk-taking and risk management in family businesses. It is based on the idea that entrepreneurial families, in addition to pursuing economic and financial objectives, attach strategic importance to intangible and affective assets, such as control, organizational identity, reputation, intergenerational continuity, and social recognition (Gómez-Mejía et al., 2007). In this perspective, risk is not assessed solely in economic terms, but rather as a potential threat to the socioemotional wealth accumulated over time. This interpretative framework is crucial, first and foremost, in the analysis of succession, where generational change is not limited to leadership but represents a moment of high symbolic value. The literature (Shen, 2018) highlights how descendant CEOs, compared to founders, exhibit greater risk aversion, preferring conservative strategies that aim to protect the SEW, even at the expense of innovation or aggressive internationalization.

In the field of corporate social responsibility (CSR), SEW provides a key to understanding the reputational motivation behind ethical and sustainable practices. According to Yang et al. (2023) and Cao et al. (2023), family businesses use CSR to consolidate their legitimacy with stakeholders, thereby protecting the family's reputation and transmitting long-term values. This behavior is particularly relevant in institutional contexts where reputation directly affects access to resources or market trust. Additionally, with respect to systemic risk, SEW helps explain the paradox that family businesses, despite being less prone to radical innovation or profound restructuring, exhibit high levels of resilience. Villagrasa et al. (2024) and Riepl et al. (2024) illustrate that, during the pandemic crisis, family businesses preferred incremental adaptation strategies to drastic actions that could have compromised internal cohesion or corporate identity. However, in the face of direct threats to SEW, the same companies demonstrate exceptional responsiveness, mobilizing capital and relational resources to safeguard continuity (Llanos-Contreras et al., 2021).

Gavana et al. (2024) integrate SEW with agency theory to explain how attachment to control and reputation can lead to earnings management practices in the presence of strong family ties. Similarly, Abdulmalik et al. (2020) show that auditors perceive lower risk in the presence of family CEOs, interpreting their commitment to protecting the business as a sign of greater reliability. In terms of performance, this focus on SEW can give rise to a form of rationality that differs from classic financial rationality: family businesses sacrifice potential economic returns to avoid decisions that jeopardize symbolic capital, as demonstrated by Mucci et al. (2022) and Abeysekera et al. (2025). These studies confirm a structural tendency to limit financial leverage, use hedging instruments, and maintain precautionary liquidity to cope with unexpected events, interpreting such behaviors as forms of risk management consistent with preserving the family legacy.

About the institutional context, SEW interacts with cultural and regulatory norms. From a comparative perspective, Li and Daspit (2016) propose a typology between 'defensive' and 'transformative' companies, where the former prioritize the preservation of SEW and the latter its strategic renegotiation through innovation or managerialization.

Regarding family reputation, Boellis et al. (2016), Park (2019), and Bansal et al. (2018) demonstrate that it is considered an extension of affective capital, the erosion of which is a primary source of perceived risk. This leads family businesses to make prudent choices in areas such as acquisitions, industrial relations, and public communication.

Finally, SEW also plays a central role in shaping compromises between innovation, risk, and generational continuity. Bornhausen and Wulf (2024) highlight how aversion to digitalization is deeply rooted in the perception that it undermines family identity and encourages excessive openness to market logic that is foreign to founding values. However, the involvement of external managers or the emergence of new generations can act as counterbalancing forces, redefining SEW's role as an evolutionary lever rather than a conservative constraint. This interpretative flexibility is also evident in Shen (2018), who proposes a dynamic perspective on SEW, according to which the perceived value of socioemotional wealth can change over time and in response to external shocks, prompting bolder strategies when SEW is perceived to be at risk.

## 3.3 Stewardship Theory

*Stewardship Theory* has become an essential lens for analyzing decision-making dynamics in family businesses, offering an alternative and complementary perspective to the classic *Agency Theory* approach. According to this perspective, family managers are not driven by opportunistic motives or selfish interests—as agency theory argues—but by a deep sense of belonging, identity values, and an orientation toward the collective good of the firm and the family (Davis et al., 1997). Contrary to the assumption that the family is always risk-averse, *Stewardship Theory* proposes that risk is taken selectively, assessed not only on economic and financial criteria but also in light of consistency with family values, intergenerational continuity, and the company's emotional mission (Le Breton-Miller & Miller, 2009). In this sense, family CEOs are viewed as "moral administrators" rather than "rational maximizers," sometimes willing to accept lower short-term performance to safeguard the company's reputation, integrity, and long-term sustainability (Eddleston & Kellermanns, 2007).

Several studies have adopted *Stewardship Theory* to explain conservative strategic decisions that are consistent with the logic of "good family governance." In this view, the lower propensity to take risks is reinterpreted as *strategic prudence* rather than a structural limitation; it represents an expression of fiduciary responsibility towards the company as a form of family wealth, intended to be passed on to future generations (Zellweger & Nason, 2008). Some research (Corbetta & Salvato, 2004) highlights how this orientation gives rise to informal yet effective governance, in which trust, value-based communication, and emotional commitment serve as alternative coordination and control mechanisms to the contractual logic of Agency Theory.

However, family leaders may hesitate to introduce radical innovations or adopt aggressive growth strategies if these threaten the company's symbolic balance or the stability of intergenerational relationships (Le Breton-Miller et al., 2011). Furthermore, the leader's strong identification with the company can lead to overcommitment, thereby increasing long-term risk exposure, particularly in the absence of formal governance structures or independent advisors (Miller et al., 2010). This is why some authors (Chrisman et al., 2015) have integrated Stewardship with other theories, such as SEW or Behavioral Agency Theory, to explain the ambivalence observed in the behavior of family businesses, which alternate between phases of caution and sudden bold decisions, especially when they perceive an existential threat to their identity.

## 3.4 Resource-Based View and Familiness

The resource-based view (RBV) is one of the main theoretical frameworks for interpreting the risk behavior of family businesses. In this context, competitive advantage derives from the possession and orchestration of resources and capabilities that are valuable, rare, difficult to imitate, and non-substitutable (Barney, 1991). In family businesses, the RBV interprets risk choices as investments aimed at developing or preserving specific intangible assets—knowledge, relationships, reputation, managerial skills—that support long-term performance.

Similarly, studies on innovation and R&D investment in family businesses use RBV to explain exposure to technological risk. In the case analyzed by Giacomarra et al. (2021), the decision to combine internal and external R&D teams in a historic family-owned winery is interpreted as a balance between transaction costs and the enhancement of internal resources, where skilled human capital, tacit knowledge, and long-term relationships become critical assets for supporting innovation while reducing the risk of project failure.

In the field of internationalization, RBV has been used to analyze how the specific resources and capabilities of family businesses influence their propensity to take risks in foreign markets. Hadryś-Nowak (2018) frames family entrepreneurship orientation—in particular, innovativeness, proactivity, and risk propensity—as a strategic resource that enables entry into and consolidation in international markets, even in the presence of constraints associated with the desire to maintain family control. In this context, the concept of familiness can be interpreted as a specific application and extension of RBV to the context of family businesses, as it aims to identify and conceptualize the particular "bundle" of resources—human and social capital, organizational culture, decision-making routines, transgenerational orientation—linked to the presence of the family in the business and capable of generating lasting competitive advantages. Familiness refers to the idiosyncratic set of resources and capabilities that arise from the systemic interaction between the family, individual members, and the business, and which distinguishes family firms from other forms of organization (Habbershon & Williams, 1999).

The literature tends to consider it primarily as a multidimensional construct rather than a complete unified theory, as while conceptual models and measurement tools have been proposed, a certain degree of ambiguity remains regarding its boundaries and nomological network, as highlighted in the review by Weismeier-Sammer et al. (2013), which warns of the risk of an overly comprehensive use of the concept and calls for its more precise theoretical and operational specification.

Theoretically, familiness has been framed primarily within the resource-based view and social capital theory, which emphasize its nature as a firm-specific resource that is difficult to imitate and rooted in relationships of trust and reciprocity among family members and between the family and stakeholders (Weismeier-Sammer et al., 2013). From this perspective, the relational and cognitive capital accumulated over time becomes a key factor in explaining the family business's ability to learn, innovate, and react to shocks, particularly in contexts of high uncertainty. At the same time, some authors have drawn on systems theory to emphasize how familiness emerges from the interaction of partially autonomous subsystems—family, business, and property—and how risk decisions are the product of decision-making patterns stabilized within these interdependent systems rather than purely individual preferences.

The use of the familiness perspective in risk studies is particularly evident in the analysis of succession processes and exogenous crises. Botella-Carrubi and González-Cruz (2019), for example, combine the resource-based view with organizational change theory to show that the risk of succession failure depends not only on formal planning for generational transition but also on the family and business contexts in which it occurs. From this perspective, the "contextual endowment" of familiness—understood as the quality of intra-family relationships, shared managerial skills, and a culture of openness to change—serves as a critical resource for addressing unexpected events and conflicts that arise during the process, thereby reducing the company's exposure to dysfunctional outcomes. A second area in which familiness is used to explain the risk profile of family businesses concerns the management of macroeconomic crises and, more generally, financial vulnerability. Villagrasa et al. (2024) interpret the financial structure choices of family firms as an expression of a combination of familiness and socioemotional wealth: the focus on continuity of lineage and the strong identification between family and business lead to prudent policies—higher levels of liquidity, lower recourse to debt, preference for self-financing—which strengthen the "financial strength" of the business and reduce its probability of default during times of crisis.

Similarly, Gómez and Rodríguez (2024) show how synergies arising from family relationships and internal social capital—central elements of familiness—can enhance strategic renewal processes in response to the COVID-19 pandemic, promoting organizational adaptation and mitigating the risks of employment vulnerability.

Familiness has also been used to interpret the ambivalence of family businesses regarding entrepreneurship and innovation, dimensions closely linked to risk appetite. Bravo Monge (2024) highlights how the structural and relational characteristics of family firms—measurable, for example, using tools such as the Family Influence Familiness Scale—can facilitate or hinder the development of a climate of corporate entrepreneurship, depending on how familiness interacts with SEW, the configuration of the top management team, and the family's attitude toward change.

In this vein, familiness can be seen both as an enabling resource, when it supports knowledge sharing and the trust necessary to undertake risky projects, and as a constraint, when it crystallizes conservative routines and aversion to strategic paths perceived as threatening to family identity.

Finally, some studies include familiness as a contextual variable in models that analyze the relationship between governance and performance, suggesting that the specific characteristics of family businesses also influence the design of control structures and, consequently, risk management. Roffia et al. (2022), for example, include familiness among the contextual forces that influence the link between board attributes and economic and financial results in SMEs, highlighting how boards of directors can be a distinctive resource, capable of strengthening risk analysis and management practices where they are consistent with the values and expectations of the owning family.

The familiness perspective, therefore, allows us to understand how the intertwining of family resources and business logic shapes the ways in which family businesses perceive, assume, and manage risk, offering an interpretative key that complements the paradigms of agency, SEW, and stewardship.

## 3.5 Legitimacy Theory

Legitimacy theory clarifies how, in family businesses, risk decisions reflect the need to preserve a recognized and respected position within the relevant institutional and social context.

It offers a complementary perspective on the risk behavior of family businesses, shifting the focus from economic objectives to the need to maintain social approval and the "permission to operate" recognized by stakeholders (Suchman, 1995). From this perspective, strategic choices, including those involving risk-taking or risk mitigation, are seen as attempts to protect and strengthen specific intangible resources of the family, such as reputation, local prestige, and socioemotional wealth. Family firms seek to comply with institutional norms and environmental expectations, including through governance choices, selective disclosure policies, and signaling strategies that aim to present the firm as legitimate, sometimes without profoundly changing operational practices. This is the direction taken, for example, by studies documenting the instrumental use of corporate social responsibility to offset earnings management practices or opportunistic behavior, thereby highlighting the risks of "hypocrisy" in family businesses (Choi et al., 2024; Lakhal et al., 2024; Alsaadi, 2022).

The link between legitimacy and risk appears intrinsically ambivalent. On the one hand, the need to preserve SEW and reputation often leads to conservative choices, aimed at reducing volatility and avoiding transactions that could compromise the family's image in the long term. The literature shows that, in many institutional contexts, family businesses adopt more prudent behaviors precisely to avoid reputational sanctions and loss of legitimacy among local communities, regulators, and markets (Sun & Wu, 2024). On the other hand, research shows that, under certain conditions, the pursuit of legitimacy can lead to greater entrepreneurial risk. Innovative investments or high-visibility projects may be deliberately pursued to strengthen the family's entrepreneurial image and consolidate its role in the socioeconomic fabric (Gundolf et al., 2013). In this sense, legitimacy acts both as a brake and as a risk-taking driver.

Risk management strategies inspired by legitimacy are also evident in governance and financial structure choices. In terms of governance, the inclusion of independent directors, the appointment of CEOs from outside the family, or the use of reputable underwriters in IPO transactions are interpreted as signaling tools aimed at reassuring markets about the soundness of control mechanisms, reducing fears of opportunism linked to family control (Ding & Pukthuanthong, 2013).

## References

Abdulmalik, S. O., Amran, N. A., & Che-Ahmad, A. (2020). Chief executive officer retirement and auditor's risk assessment: The interacting effect of chief executive officer identity in family firms. *Journal of Financial Reporting and Accounting, 18*(2), 343–361.

Abeysekera, A. P., Brockman, P., Fernando, C. S., & Salas, J. M. (2025). Undiversified shareholders, socioemotional wealth, and corporate hedging: Evidence from family firms. *International Review of Financial Analysis, 102*, 104092.

Abid, A., Shaique, M., & Anwar ul Haq, M. (2018). Do big four auditors always provide higher audit quality? Evidence from Pakistan. *International Journal of Financial Studies, 6*(2), 58.

Acero, I., & Alcalde, N. (2016). Controlling shareholders and the composition of the board: special focus on family firms. *Review of Managerial Science, 10*, 61–83.

Al Maani, A., Buraik, O., Al-Amarneh, A., & Almashaqbeh, M. (2025). The effect of the audit committee on the voluntary risk disclosure in Jordanian commercial banks: The moderating role of family ownership. *Journal of Risk and Financial Management, 18*(3), 133.

Alessandri, T. M., Cerrato, D., & Eddleston, K. A. (2018). The mixed gamble of internationalization in family and nonfamily firms: The moderating role of organizational slack. *Global Strategy Journal, 8*(1), 46–72.

Alsaadi, A. (2022). Family ownership and corporate social responsibility disclosure. *Spanish Journal of Finance and Accounting/Revista Española de Financiación y Contabilidad, 51*(2), 160–182.

Alshirah, M. H., Rahman, A. A., & Mustapa, I. R. (2020). Board of directors' characteristics and corporate risk disclosure: The moderating role of family ownership. *EuroMed Journal of Business, 15*(2), 219–252.

Anderson, R. C., Duru, A., & Reeb, D. M. (2009). Founders, heirs, and corporate opacity in the United States. *Journal of Financial Economics, 92*(2), 205–222.

Baek, H. Y., Cho, D. D., & Fazio, P. L. (2016). Family ownership, control and corporate capital structure: An examination of small capitalization public firms. *Journal of Family Business Management, 6*(2), 169–185.

Bansal, S., Lopez-Perez, M. V., & Rodriguez-Ariza, L. (2018). Board independence and corporate social responsibility disclosure: The mediating role of the presence of family ownership. *Administrative Sciences, 8*(3), 33.

Barney, J. (1991). Firm resources and sustained competitive advantage. *Journal of Management, 17*(1), 99–120.

Berrone, P., Cruz, C., & Gomez-Mejia, L. R. (2012). Socioemotional wealth in family firms: Theoretical dimensions, assessment approaches, and agenda for future research. *Family Business Review, 25*(3), 258–279.

Block, J. H. (2012). R&D investments in family and founder firms: An agency perspective. *Journal of Business Venturing, 27*(2), 248–265.

Bodnaruk, A., Massa, M., & Yadav, V. (2017). Family ownership, country governance, and foreign portfolio investment. *Journal of Empirical Finance, 41*, 96–115.

Boellis, A., Mariotti, S., Minichilli, A., & Piscitello, L. (2016). Family involvement and firms' establishment mode choice in foreign markets. *Journal of International Business Studies, 47*, 929–950.

Bornhausen, A. M., & Wulf, T. (2024). Digital innovation in family firms: The roles of non-family managers and transgenerational control intentions. *Small Business Economics, 62*(4), 1429–1448.

Botella-Carrubi, M. D., & González-Cruz, T. F. (2019). Context as a provider of key resources for succession: A case study of sustainable family firms. *Sustainability, 11*(7), 1873.

Boubaker, S., Nguyen, P., & Rouatbi, W. (2016). Multiple large shareholders and corporate risk-taking: Evidence from French family firms. *European Financial Management, 22*(4), 697–745.

Bravo Monge, C. (2024). Corporate entrepreneurship and family businesses: A perspective article. *Journal of Family Business Management, 14*(6), 1227–1233.

Cao, F., Li, S., Dai, M., & Li, J. (2023). Your heart is where your treasure is: Family chairman and tax avoidance in family-controlled firms. *Journal of Business Research, 154*, 113298.

Choi, J., Roh, T., & Lee, J. H. (2024). The pitfalls of corporate social irresponsibility: Hypocrisy of family firms in South Korea. *Journal of Cleaner Production, 435*, 140557.

Chrisman, J. J., Chua, J. H., De Massis, A., Frattini, F., & Wright, M. (2015). The ability and willingness paradox in family firm innovation. *Journal of Product Innovation Management, 32*(3), 310–318.

Corbetta, G., & Salvato, C. (2004). Self–serving or self–actualizing? Models of man and agency costs in different types of family firms: A commentary on "comparing the agency costs of family and non–family firms: Conceptual issues and exploratory evidence". *Entrepreneurship Theory and Practice, 28*(4), 355–362.

Davis, J. H., Schoorman, F. D., & Donaldson, L. (1997). Toward a stewardship theory of management. *Academy of Management Review, 22*(1), 20–47.

D'Este, C., & Carabelli, M. (2022). Family ownership and risk: The role of family managers. *Corporate Governance: The International Journal of Business in Society, 22*(6), 1161–1177.

Ding, H. B., & Pukthuanthong, K. (2013). Legitimacy signals and family IPO performances. *Journal of Business Economics and Management, 14*(1), 156–181.

Eddleston, K. A., & Kellermanns, F. W. (2007). Destructive and productive family relationships: A stewardship theory perspective. *Journal of Business Venturing, 22*(4), 545–565.

Gavana, G., Gottardo, P., & Moisello, A. M. (2024). Related party transactions and earnings management in family firms: The moderating role of board characteristics. *Journal of Family Business Management, 14*(1), 171–198.

George, G. (2005). Slack resources and the performance of privately held firms. *Academy of Management Journal, 48*(4), 661–676.

Giacomarra, M., Shams, S. R., Crescimanno, M., Sakka, G., Gregori, G. L., & Galati, A. (2021). Internal vs. external R&D teams: Evidences from the Italian wine industry. *Journal of Business Research, 128*, 752–761.

Gómez-Mejía, L. R., Haynes, K. T., Núñez-Nickel, M., Jacobson, K. J., & Moyano-Fuentes, J. (2007). Socioemotional wealth and business risks in family-controlled firms: Evidence from Spanish olive oil mills. *Administrative Science Quarterly, 52*(1), 106–137.

Gómez, J. M., & Rodríguez, Y. E. (2024). Strategic renewal of family firms to face vulnerability risks during times of crisis. *International Journal of Social Economics, 51*(12), 1538–1564.

Gundolf, K., Meier, O., & Missonier, A. (2013). Transmission of family businesses in France. *International Journal of Entrepreneurial Behavior & Research, 19*(1), 53–71.

Habbershon, T. G., & Williams, M. L. (1999). A resource-based framework for assessing the strategic advantages of family firms. *Family Business Review, 12*(1), 1–25.

Hadryś-Nowak, A. (2018). Family entrepreneurship orientation in family owned SMEs: A key resource for internationalization? *Entrepreneurial Business and Economics Review, 6*(2), 153–169.

Ismail, R. F., Arshad, R., & Othman, S. (2014). The influence of insider ownership and board independence on the narrative risk reporting. *Asian Social Science, 10*(1), 28.

Lakhal, F., Ben Saad, I., Lakhal, N., & Gaaya, S. (2024). How do socially responsible companies engage in tax avoidance practices? Evidence from France. *Management International/ International Management/Gestiòn Internacional, 28*(5).

La Rosa, F., Bernini, F., & Verona, R. (2020). Ownership structure and the cost of equity in the European context: The mediating effect of earnings management. *Meditari Accountancy Research, 28*(3), 485–514.

Le Breton-Miller, I., & Miller, D. (2009). Agency vs. stewardship in public family firms: A social embeddedness reconciliation. *Entrepreneurship Theory and Practice, 33*(6), 1169–1191.

Le Breton-Miller, I., Miller, D., & Lester, R. H. (2011). Stewardship or agency? A social embeddedness reconciliation of conduct and performance in public family businesses. *Organization Science, 22*(3), 704–721.

Li, Z., & Daspit, J. J. (2016). Understanding family firm innovation heterogeneity: A typology of family governance and socioemotional wealth intentions. *Journal of Family Business Management, 6*(2), 103–121.

Llanos-Contreras, O., Arias, J., & Maquieira, C. (2021). Risk taking behavior in Chilean listed family firms: A socioemotional wealth approach. *International Entrepreneurship and Management Journal, 17*(1), 165–184.

Martínez-Ferrero, J., Rodríguez-Ariza, L., & García-Sánchez, I. M. (2016). Corporate social responsibility as an entrenchment strategy, with a focus on the implications of family ownership. *Journal of Cleaner Production, 135*, 760–770.

Meckling, W. H., & Jensen, M. C. (1976). Theory of the firm. *Managerial behavior, Agency Costs and Ownership Structure, 3*(4), 305–360.
Meier, O., & Thelisson, A. S. (2020). The succession dilemma in family firms: Case study of a French company. *Journal of Business Strategy, 42*(6), 406–411.
Miller, D., Le Breton-Miller, I., & Lester, R. H. (2010). Family ownership and acquisition behavior in publicly-traded companies. *Strategic Management Journal, 31*(2), 201–223.
Mucci, D. M., Beck, F., & Ferrari, A. (2022). Socioemotional wealth and entrepreneurial orientation in different family businesses' generational stages. *BAR-Brazilian Administration Review, 19*(02), e210053.
Park, S. B. (2019). Family leadership and CSR decoupling: Founder–descendant differences in socioemotional wealth. *BRQ Business Research Quarterly, 23409444241289146.*
Riepl, J., Mitter, C., & Kuttner, M. (2024). Risk management during the COVID-19 crisis: Insights from an exploratory case study of medium-sized family businesses. *Journal of Management Control, 35*(1), 109–135.
Roffia, P., Simón-Moya, V., & Sendra García, J. (2022). Board of director attributes: Effects on financial performance in SMEs. *International Entrepreneurship and Management Journal, 18*(3), 1141–1172.
Saghi-Zedek, N., & Tarazi, A. (2015). Excess control rights, financial crisis and bank profitability and risk. *Journal of Banking & Finance, 55*, 361–379.
Shahzad, A., Nazir, M. S., Morais, F., & Asghar Butt, A. (2025). Ownership structure, board composition and CEO dominance: What does really matters to corporate deleveraging policies? *Corporate Governance: The International Journal of Business in Society, 25*(4), 786–814.
Shen, N. (2018). Family business, transgenerational succession and diversification strategy: Implication from a dynamic socioemotional wealth model. *Cross Cultural & Strategic Management, 25*(4), 628–641.
Suchman, M. C. (1995). Managing legitimacy: Strategic and institutional approaches. *Academy of Management Review, 20*(3), 571–610.
Sun, Y., & Wu, Z. (2024). Reputational risk and firm performance: Family versus nonfamily firms in different regulatory environments. *Journal of International Financial Markets, Institutions and Money, 93*, 101976.
Villagrasa, J., Escribá-Esteve, A., Donaldson, C., & Sánchez-Peinado, E. (2024). Firms financial strength during crisis periods: Does "familiness" matter? *Journal of Family Business Management*. https://doi.org/10.1108/jfbm-02-2024-0042
Weismeier-Sammer, D., Frank, H., & von Schlippe, A. (2013). Untangling 'familiness' A literature review and directions for future research. *The International Journal of Entrepreneurship and Innovation, 14*(3), 165–177.
Wiseman, R. M., & Gomez-Mejia, L. R. (1998). A behavioral agency model of managerial risk taking. *Academy of Management Review, 23*(1), 133–153.
Yang, M., Wang, Y., Bai, L., & Maresova, P. (2023). Corporate social responsibility, family involvement, and stock price crash risk. *Corporate Social Responsibility and Environmental Management, 30*(3), 1204–1225.
Zahra, S. A. (2005). Entrepreneurial risk taking in family firms. *Family Business Review, 18*(1), 23–40.
Zellweger, T. M., & Nason, R. S. (2008). A stakeholder perspective on family firm performance. *Family Business Review, 21*(3), 203–216.

# Chapter 4
# Governance, Ownership Structure, and Risk in Family Businesses

**Abstract** This chapter examines the role of governance in risk management and value creation within family businesses, drawing on two complementary perspectives.

On the one hand, the analysis focuses on the structural characteristics of governance–ownership configurations, board composition, and information transparency, in line with the cluster dedicated to "ownership structure, board structure, and risk (blue)." Through an institutional and organizational perspective, it examines how concentrated ownership structures, overlap between ownership and control, voting mechanisms, and disclosure practices affect risk perception and management. The composition of the board of directors emerges as a decisive lever for balancing family interests with governance effectiveness. At the same time, the degree of transparency directly affects the trust of external stakeholders.

On the other hand, the link between "governance, risk, and performance" (orange cluster) is explored in depth, highlighting how the family nature of the company can be both a competitive advantage and a source of vulnerability. Risk appetite is shaped by relational, institutional, and generational factors, often translating into conservative strategies that prioritize protecting socioemotional wealth and a long-term vision. However, the absence of professional governance and transparency in information can reduce competitiveness, limiting the company's ability to adapt to external shocks.

**Keywords** Corporate governance · Ownership concentration · Board structure · Independent directors · Agency conflicts · Risk

## 4.1 Ownership Structure and Risk

The ownership structure of family businesses plays a decisive—and often ambivalent—role in defining risk management strategies. The concentration of wealth within the family and the centrality of socioemotional wealth (SEW) typically lead to a cautious approach, which manifests as a greater propensity to hedge market



A. M. Moisello, P. Gottardo, *Risk and Sustainability in Family Businesses*, SpringerBriefs in Finance, https://doi.org/10.1007/978-3-032-19995-9_4

risks, especially when the CEO is a founder or a direct family member (Abeysekera et al., 2025). In various contexts, this attitude is associated with lower exposure to default risk (Abinzano et al., 2021) and more moderate use of financial leverage, consistent with risk aversion (Al-Ajmi et al., 2009; Anderson et al., 2012). However, the relationship between ownership and risk management is not straightforward: in small US firms, for example, family ownership is associated with greater use of leverage, but only when the family does not also hold operational control, highlighting the crucial role of the overlap between ownership and control (Baek et al., 2016).

In emerging and institutionally fragile contexts, family ownership is often associated with conservative choices, such as limiting cross-border acquisitions (Chen et al., 2009) or accumulating excess liquidity (Parrado-Martínez et al., 2024), which can sometimes come at the expense of growth and capital efficiency. On the other hand, the presence of multiple large shareholders tends to offset the conservative family orientation, promoting greater risk-taking and reducing agency costs (Attig et al., 2013). In bank-based environments, such as Austria, the greater availability of credit enables family businesses to utilize more debt while maintaining quicker control over leverage in the event of changes in the financial environment (Burgstaller & Wagner, 2015).

Voting mechanisms also play a key role. Companies with dual-class share structures reduce their use of debt and financial hedging to avoid dilution of control (Hagelin et al., 2006), while the adoption of pyramid structures appears to be a strategy to contain the cost of family under-diversification (Heaney & Holmen, 2008). In countries with weak investor protection, the combination of high ownership concentration and gaps between voting and cash rights increases lenders' perceived risk, thereby raising the cost of debt (Boubakri & Ghouma, 2010). However, the reputation of founding families, as evidenced in GCC countries, can mitigate the adverse effects of practices such as related-party transactions (Eulaiwi et al., 2023).

Other studies reveal more complex and non-linear dynamics. In Korea, for example, risk appetite has a U-shaped relationship with family ownership, with intermediate levels associated with greater caution and high levels related to bolder investments (Lee et al., 2018). In India, leverage in family business groups grows to a certain point and then declines, reflecting a trade-off between growth and power preservation (Chakraborty, 2018). In Spain, the relationship between ownership concentration and risk exhibits a nonlinear pattern (Otero-González et al., 2022), with lower risk when family ownership is either very high or very low.

On the other hand, it has been shown that hedging strategies, when adopted by founders, may reflect a personal interest in asset protection rather than a logic of maximizing enterprise value (Kim et al., 2014). Furthermore, in the presence of earnings management, ownership structure can increase the cost of capital, despite the perceived alignment effect in the market (La Rosa et al., 2020). Finally, board composition can moderate the impact of ownership on risk, as evidence indicates that greater gender diversity reduces the propensity to adopt zero-leverage policies, favoring a more balanced approach (Shahzad et al., 2025).

## 4.2 Board Characteristics and Risk

In contexts characterized by high ownership concentration, such as family-owned businesses, the composition of the board assumes strategic importance in balancing the interests of majority and minority shareholders. Increasing the proportion of independent directors is often used to mitigate type II agency conflicts, that is, the expropriation of minority shareholders by controlling shareholders (Acero & Alcalde, 2016). However, the very presence of family members on the board can limit the effective independence of control bodies, as demonstrated by Alhababsah and Azzam (2024), who find that family ownership mitigates the effectiveness of audit committees in promoting risk disclosure.

Another critical dimension is CEO duality, which is often found in family businesses and is associated with lower transparency and a higher risk of entrenchment, unless it is offset by experienced and diverse boards (Alshirah et al., 2020). Even with formally competent boards, the family can still limit disclosure to preserve SEW, as highlighted by Alshirah et al. (2022). Similar dynamics emerge in the context of strong political ties, where family control can either mitigate or amplify opportunism, depending on the quality of the board (Baig et al., 2024).

The presence of effective board configurations—such as those identified by Brogi et al. (2021), including active independent boards with strengthened internal controls and greater female representation—reduces the risk of opportunistic use of liquidity and improves the protection of minority shareholders. Furthermore, board size and independence limit excessive cash accumulation (Guizani et al., 2018) and strengthen crisis preparedness (Faghfouri et al., 2015).

In contexts characterized by dual class shares or strong voting rights, such as France, the absence of an adequate proportion of independent directors amplifies information opacity and disclosure risks (Ali, 2014). Furthermore, earnings management practices or risky decisions may emerge when the board lacks diversity or is overly controlled by the family (Gavana et al., 2024). The introduction of external CFOs and the presence of non-family investors can, on the other hand, foster a more sophisticated and neutral approach to risk management (Di Giuli et al., 2011).

The issue of diversity—in terms of gender, role, or skills—is also crucial: the presence of independent women on the board increases entrepreneurial risk-taking in a virtuous way, while non-independent women reinforce conservative and defensive behaviors linked to the protection of the SEW (Poletti-Hughes & Briano-Turrent, 2019). Finally, evidence indicates that the introduction of external CEOs can alter a company's risk strategies, but this effect is mediated by both the control exercised through the board and the CEO's tenure (Lardon et al., 2017; Huybrechts et al., 2013).

Finally, financial engineering tools such as tenure-based voting rights (TVRs) enable families to access capital without relinquishing control, thereby encouraging investment and mitigating the risks of underinvestment (Imperatore & Pope, 2024). However, distortive control structures, such as the wedge between voting and cash rights, can reduce market value and protect the family from hostile takeovers, thereby hindering effective risk management (Holmen & Nivorozhkin, 2007).

Overall, the characteristics of boards in family businesses are central to tensions between preservation and openness, control and professionalization, and the balance among independence, expertise, transparency, and family involvement is crucial for effective risk management.

## 4.3 Risk Disclosure and Transparency

Evidence shows that family businesses tend, on average, to disclose less risk voluntarily than their non-family counterparts, especially in emerging countries where the family directly controls the board of directors (Alshirah & Alshirah'h, 2024). This behavior reflects a conservative approach aimed at mitigating negative market reactions and minimizing the visibility of potential vulnerabilities.

The presence of independent directors, institutional shareholders, or larger non-family shareholders improves transparency and promotes more advanced disclosure practices (Attig et al., 2013; Salem et al., 2019). In the context of political ties, such as those in GCC countries, good governance mitigates the adverse effects of family and political connections on risk disclosure (Al-Hadi et al., 2018). The presence of accountability and CSR practices also strengthens the legitimacy of family businesses, reducing perceived uncertainty (Alsaadi, 2024).

On the auditing front, family businesses are generally perceived as less risky by auditors, who charge lower fees and devote less effort to auditing them because of their lower propensity for information manipulation (Abudy et al., 2024). However, this trust may be unfounded in markets with weak enforcement, where even high-quality auditors struggle to curb earnings management practices (Abid et al., 2018). In addition, weak audit committees or committees that are formally independent but substantially linked to the family compromise the effectiveness of controls (Krishnan & Peytcheva, 2019).

In emerging economies, family culture is a significant determinant. In Brazilian companies, it fosters structured risk management practices and transparent disclosure (Brandt et al., 2021). In contrast, in China and other Asian contexts, the focus on safeguarding socioemotional wealth leads to the avoidance of opportunistic behavior, including aggressive tax avoidance (Cao et al., 2023).

Corporate governance mechanisms moderate the impact of family control on information quality and risk perception. The presence of former CEOs on the board reduces audit costs (Cai et al., 2023), while more balanced ownership structures improve bond ratings (Oh et al., 2022). However, excessive family control, especially when voting rights are misaligned with economic rights, increases volatility and perceived risk, unless propping-up behavior intervenes to support stability in times of crisis (Saghi-Zedek & Tarazi, 2015).

In the fiscal and legal spheres, family businesses exhibit a greater propensity to comply, especially when they perceive high reputational risks, as is the case with politically connected Spanish companies (Bona-Sánchez et al., 2020). At the same time, a focus on transparency can also stem from cultural factors: for example, in Italy, regional religiosity helps to strengthen creditor confidence and reduce the likelihood of credit rationing (Peruzzi, 2024).

## 4.4 The Relationship Between Risk and Performance

The performance of family businesses has been the subject of extensive debate in economic and business literature, with often ambivalent results reflecting the variety of family structures, institutional contexts, and stages of the business life cycle. Unlike non-family businesses, family businesses are characterized by a broader set of objectives that include not only economic outcomes but also the preservation of socioemotional heritage, generational continuity, and family reputation (Berrone et al., 2012). These specificities have a significant impact on risk management and, consequently, business performance.

Numerous studies confirm that family businesses, under certain conditions, outperform their non-family counterparts. This is the case, for example, of companies led by co-founders, where the distribution of leadership reduces the risk of dependence on a single top figure, making governance more balanced and resilient (Baek & Kim, 2015). In contexts where family control is accompanied by professional management, as noted by Gama and Galvão (2012), family businesses exhibit higher levels of performance. However, overly concentrated mechanisms—such as the adoption of double-class shares—can generate risks of expropriation of minority shareholders, with adverse effects on enterprise value.

However, in weak institutional environments, such as Mexico, the presence of family CEOs is associated with poorer performance, unless these leaders have adequate management training to compensate for structural deficiencies in the operating environment (Watkins-Fassler et al., 2019). The quality of information provided to markets also plays a crucial role as greater readability of annual reports, regardless of ownership structure, significantly reduces the risk of stock market crashes, highlighting the importance of information transparency for business stability (Shandiz et al., 2022).

Some empirical evidence suggests that family businesses tend to be more conservative in their financial management, typically maintaining higher liquidity levels. While this can act as a buffer in turbulent times, it also implies a discount on the marginal value of cash, particularly when heirs run the business, suggesting potential inefficiencies in the management of liquid assets (Caprio et al., 2020). Intergenerational dynamics are a key factor because, in subsequent generations, emotional capital can become rigid and resistant to change, with negative effects on performance (Gottardo & Moisello, 2015).

Family involvement in management also has different effects. McConaughy et al. (2001) find that companies controlled by the founding family are generally more efficient, enjoy better alignment between ownership and control, and reduce agency costs. More recent studies suggest that, in young SMEs, family ownership and activism increase profitability, whereas in more mature companies they can constrain growth and strategic adaptation (Lwango et al., 2017).

In the context of rural tourism businesses, innovativeness and proactivity have been identified as key determinants of performance, whereas risk propensity is less significant (Kallmuenzer & Peters, 2018). This observation aligns with a broader view that individual variables cannot explain the performance of family businesses; rather, it is the result of the interaction between different elements, including entrepreneurial orientation, succession intentions, family involvement, and the ability to take and manage risks (Kraus et al., 2018).

Finally, the company's size and age are additional factors in discrimination. According to Miralles-Marcelo et al. (2014), small family businesses with a long history tend to perform better, thanks to a strong sense of identity and a desire for continuity. Conversely, in larger or younger companies, the competitive advantages of family businesses tend to diminish, approaching the levels of non-family businesses. Similarly, Poletti-Hughes and Williams (2019) demonstrate that the desire to preserve socioemotional wealth can prompt families to undertake greater risk, but only within certain limits of ownership concentration.

Overall, the studies examined show that the performance of family businesses results from a dynamic balance among structural, relational, and institutional factors. Family governance can be a competitive advantage in highly uncertain contexts, but only if accompanied by professionalization, information transparency, and strategic adaptability. In this context, risk management emerges not as an ancillary variable, but as an integral element of the family business model's specificities.

## 4.5 Conservative Strategies and Idiosyncratic Risk Management

Several studies have shown that the propensity for conservative strategies, on the one hand, serves as a form of protection against instability, and, on the other, may constrain the optimization of enterprise value. In highly volatile contexts, as documented by Chen and Wang (2019) in the Taiwanese case, family businesses can adopt innovative strategies, investing more heavily in R&D, thanks to their in-depth knowledge of the industry and long-term vision, consistent with the 'real options' approach. However, this ability to exploit opportunities is constrained by market perceptions: Ferreira et al. (2025) show that, in Brazil, although idiosyncratic risk increases the value of cash, this effect is attenuated in family businesses, suggesting that their financial caution reduces investor recognition of value.

On the third-party capital front, Canbaloglu et al. (2022) find that the use of long-term debt can contribute to stock price stability in family businesses, where internal monitoring mitigates agency conflicts, favoring more balanced financial structures. However, evidence from Huang and Chan (2013) indicates that excessive leverage, in the absence of adequate governance, can compromise performance, especially in financially risky firms. In fact, independent boards and CEOs with dual roles are associated with better results, suggesting the importance of a structured corporate governance framework.

In terms of transparency, Lee et al. (2024) demonstrate that voluntary disclosure of environmental information is an effective conservative strategy, particularly for non-conglomerate family businesses, which achieve a greater reduction in the risk of stock collapse than Korean chaebols. In the context of international financial policies, Mefteh-Wali and Hussain (2024) highlight that family businesses' currency-hedging practices are often ineffective and do not create value, as they prioritize protecting family wealth over the interests of minority shareholders.

The lack of asset diversification typical of family shareholdings, as observed by Roger and Schatt (2016), leads to greater exposure to idiosyncratic risk, prompting owners to demand private benefits that penalize market valuation. Rajverma et al. (2019) confirm that, in emerging markets, ownership concentration and opaque dividend policy amplify idiosyncratic risk, while greater distributional transparency can act as a corrective mechanism. The power structure also significantly affects the risk profile: Tran et al. (2023) show that in Vietnamese family businesses, CEO-chair dualism increases the probability of a stock crash unless the CEO holds a significant shareholding, thereby aligning interests.

A sound governance system, including dedicated committees, adequate skills, and structured risk analysis processes, is crucial for improving performance and reducing vulnerability among family SMEs (Roffia et al., 2022). Similarly, Wu et al. (2020) find that in Taiwan, board transparency and independence reduce the risk of share price collapse, particularly in family businesses, where conflicts of interest are structurally more pronounced. However, a strong presence of short-term-oriented institutional investors can exacerbate volatility, undermining the stability sought by families.

Finally, Watkins-Fassler et al. (2019) note that family ownership alone is insufficient to ensure effective risk management. In weak institutional environments, companies led by family CEOs who lack the necessary managerial skills exhibit greater volatility and poorer performance, underscoring that conservative strategies can yield positive effects only when supported by adequate technical capabilities and governance tools.

## 4.6 Agency Conflicts, Transparency, and Governance Quality

In family businesses, agency conflicts are a critical dimension of risk management, as the overlap between ownership and control does not necessarily eliminate opportunistic behavior; instead, it transforms it. Recent literature has highlighted that governance structures, information transparency, and the balance of risk appetite are central to mitigating the distortions generated by such conflicts. Ali et al. (2025) demonstrate that the inclusion of externally co-opted female directors enhances the value of family businesses by improving governance quality and enhancing risk management, thereby supporting agency theory, which posits that diversified governance reduces the distance between ownership and management.

On the other hand, Chaabouni et al. (2025) document that in Saudi Arabia, board independence and high ESG scores are associated with worse performance, especially in family businesses, where intense ownership concentration hinders the effectiveness of independent directors, thereby increasing agency risks. Complementarily, Rodríguez et al. (2021) observe that risk orientation (RTO) has a non-linear relationship with performance. While excessive risk aversion reduces performance, an overly high propensity to take risks does not necessarily improve it, suggesting that governance effectiveness depends on balancing socioemotional goals with economic rationality.

The role of transparency emerges strongly in the studies by Haj-Salem et al. (2020) and Shandiz et al. (2022): the former highlights that high disclosure can only replace other control tools if accompanied by effective governance; the latter demonstrates that greater readability of annual reports limits the accumulation of bad news and reduces the risk of sudden stock price crashes, acting as an information risk reduction device. In this context, the independence of the board of directors also plays a decisive role: Wu et al. (2020) emphasize that large and independent boards act as a brake on opportunistic behavior, reducing the risk of reputational and financial crises.

Cognitive and motivational dynamics further complicate the relationship between risk propensity and future performance. According to Mahto and Khanin (2015), satisfaction with past results tends to reduce openness to risk, while a greater propensity for risk raises expectations of future results. This ambivalence is also analyzed by Srinidhi and Liao (2020), who propose a distinction between the "alignment effect," which reduces the risk of stock crashes thanks to the family's long-term vision, and the "entrenchment effect," according to which family managers may conceal negative news, increasing the vulnerability of the company.

Other studies emphasize that risk management must go beyond formal structures alone. Rasheed et al. (2025) find that family presence on the board alone does not reduce the risk of stock market crashes, while the absence of active monitoring by institutional investors can exacerbate agency conflicts. In this vein, Pelaez-Leon and Sanchez-Marin (2022) show that human resource management policies, such as training and motivation, effectively mediate the relationship between socioemotional goals (SEW) and financial performance, reducing risk when well integrated but increasing vulnerability when SEW is used as an isolated strategic guide.

Finally, Kotey et al. (2019) highlight that listed family businesses earn 30% less than non-family businesses, precisely because of the growing separation between ownership and management, which leads to the re-emergence of classic agency conflicts. However, the presence of foreign investors can improve profitability, suggesting that greater openness and inclusive governance can contribute to more effective risk management.

## 4.7 Critical Reflections on the Relationship Between Family Governance and Risk

Considering the theoretical and empirical evidence examined, this section provides a critical summary of the key aspects that have emerged, articulating the discussion along the two thematic lines on which the chapter focuses.

The first subsection examines the relationship among ownership structure, board composition, and risk management, highlighting how institutional and organizational configurations shape the risk profile of family firms and the quality of governance. The second focuses on the relationship between governance, risk, and performance, emphasizing the conditions under which family identity serves as either a strategic lever or a constraint for value creation.

### *4.7.1 Critical Analysis: Ownership Structure, Board Structure, and Risk*

The presence of family members in the capital and in company management has a profound influence on risk management, promoting a long-term orientation and strategic caution, often linked to the protection of socioemotional wealth. This translates into prudent behavior such as limiting debt (Anderson et al., 2012) and a lower propensity to manipulate earnings, which improves the perceived quality of accounting information and reduces audit costs (Abudy et al., 2024). Furthermore, founding families can act as reputational guarantors, particularly in unstable contexts, actively supporting the company during crises (Saghi-Zedek & Tarazi, 2015).

This implies that family ownership stability can act as a risk buffer, but only if supported by conscious, rather than merely defensive, management.

The composition of the board of directors plays a crucial role. Diverse and professional boards—with independent members, female representation, and non-family members—improve governance quality, promote transparency, and enhance innovation and adaptation capabilities (Ali et al., 2025; Cai et al., 2023; Poletti-Hughes & Briano-Turrent, 2019).

For family businesses, this highlights the opportunity to structure inclusive and pluralistic boards as a lever to mitigate risk and strengthen external legitimacy.

However, in the absence of adequate separation between ownership and control, significant vulnerabilities remain. Highly concentrated ownership structures, pyramidal arrangements, and dual-class shares reduce transparency and can inhibit adequate supervision (Holmen & Nivorozhkin, 2007; Hagelin et al., 2006). In these contexts, risk disclosure tends to be limited and selective, both to avoid adverse market reactions and to mask internal fragilities (Alshirah and Alshira'h, 2024; Al Maani et al., 2025).

This evidence suggests that the protection afforded by family control, if not balanced by accountability and transparent communication, can increase stakeholders' perception of risk and compromise efficient access to capital.

The weakness of audit committees, which are often formal and not truly independent, also limits monitoring capabilities and exacerbates information risk (Krishnan & Peytcheva, 2019).

As a result, strengthening internal control mechanisms must not be merely formal but substantial, aiming to ensure competence, autonomy, and credibility.

Generational transitions are another critical juncture. Assigning top roles to family members who lack adequate skills or are selected for dynastic reasons reduces decision-making efficiency and increases exposure to strategic and reputational risks (Gottardo & Moisello, 2015). Furthermore, heirs may adopt conservative strategies that, in the absence of a forward-looking approach, lead to rigidity and loss of competitiveness (Caprio et al., 2020).

These findings suggest an urgent need for selection and succession processes based on meritocratic and professional criteria, so that family continuity does not compromise the business's agility and capacity for innovation.

Family businesses, therefore, have unique levers for risk management, linked to continuity, cohesion, and direct control. However, these advantages can easily turn into sources of fragility if not accompanied by transparent, inclusive, and professional governance.

Effective risk management, therefore, requires an integrated view of choices regarding ownership structure, board composition, and disclosure quality, recognizing these as interdependent strategic components for the long-term sustainability of the company.

### *4.7.2 Critical Analysis: Resilience and Fragility in Risk Management*

One of the main strengths of family businesses in risk management lies in their long-term vision, which often guides patient strategies aimed at preserving continuity and socioemotional capital (Gottardo & Moisello, 2015; Poletti-Hughes & Williams, 2019). This orientation is reflected in conservative practices, such as maintaining high levels of liquidity and low financial leverage (McConaughy et al., 2001; Caprio et al., 2020), which serve as protective buffers during times of turbulence.

Such strategies imply a comparative advantage in highly uncertain contexts, provided they are supported by sound governance and competent leadership.

Indeed, when supported by professionalization processes and adequate decision-making structures, these practices are associated with lower exposure to idiosyncratic risk (Chen & Wang, 2019) and greater organizational resilience (Watkins-Fassler et al., 2019). However, the same elements that promote stability can degenerate into operational rigidity. Excessive caution, often motivated by a desire to preserve family control, can reduce the propensity to innovate and hinder growth (Ferreira et al., 2025; Kraus et al., 2018).

This highlights the need to strike a balance between managerial prudence and an entrepreneurial culture that is more open to strategic risk and investment.

Concentrated ownership structures and poor asset diversification, typical of many family businesses, increase exposure to specific risks and reduce asset market valuation (Rajverma et al., 2019). At the same time, ineffective hedging strategies or those driven by secondary agency conflicts can compromise financial risk management (Mefteh-Wali & Hussain, 2024).

To mitigate these vulnerabilities, it is advisable to introduce independent control mechanisms and managerial tools for risk assessment and management geared toward long-term performance.

The quality of family governance is also a key factor. The absence of independent boards or committees specifically dedicated to risk supervision is associated with greater exposure to adverse events, especially in fragile institutional contexts (Wu et al., 2020; Roffia et al., 2022).

This suggests the importance of equipping family businesses with governing bodies comprised of qualified external figures who can counterbalance family power and enhance market confidence.

At the same time, risk disclosure plays a crucial role. Although transparency is often limited in family businesses, particularly in emerging contexts, it can serve as a substitute for or as a complement to formal governance when credible and supported by effective control structures (Haj-Salem et al., 2020). The presence of independent directors, active institutional investors, and professional boards is associated with improved information disclosure quality (Attig et al., 2013; Al-Hadi et al., 2018).

Consequently, the adoption of structured and verifiable disclosure practices is a strategic lever for reducing reputational risk and improving market valuation.

Finally, the resilience of family businesses is not so much a structural feature as the result of a dynamic balance between continuity and openness, preservation and innovation (Pelaez-Leon & Sanchez-Marin, 2022; Mahto & Khanin, 2015). This balance must be built over time through investment in organizational culture, training of new generations, and professionalization of governance.

## References

Abeysekera, A. P., Brockman, P., Fernando, C. S., & Salas, J. M. (2025). Undiversified shareholders, socioemotional wealth, and corporate hedging: Evidence from family firms. *International Review of Financial Analysis, 102*, 104092.

Abid, A., Shaique, M., & Anwar ul Haq, M. (2018). Do big four auditors always provide higher audit quality? Evidence from Pakistan. *International Journal of Financial Studies, 6*(2), 58.

Abinzano, I., Corredor, P., & Martinez, B. (2021). Does family ownership always reduce default risk? *Accounting & Finance, 61*(3), 4025–4060.

Abudy, M., Amir, E., & Shust, E. (2024). Are family firms less audit-risky? Analysing audit fees, hours and rates. *Accounting and Business Research*, 1–27.

Acero, I., & Alcalde, N. (2016). Controlling shareholders and the composition of the board: special focus on family firms. *Review of Managerial Science, 10*, 61–83.

Al Maani, A., Buraik, O., Al-Amarneh, A., & Almashaqbeh, M. (2025). The effect of the audit committee on the voluntary risk disclosure in Jordanian commercial banks: The moderating role of family ownership. *Journal of Risk and Financial Management, 18*(3), 133.

Al-Ajmi, J., Hussain, H. A., & Al-Saleh, N. (2009). Decisions on capital structure in a Zakat environment with prohibition of riba: The case of Saudi Arabia. *The Journal of Risk Finance, 10*(5), 460–476.

Alhababsah, S., & Azzam, A. A. (2024). On the independence of audit committee in developing countries: Evidence from Jordan. *Journal of Applied Accounting Research, 25*(5), 1203–1222.

Al-Hadi, A., Al-Yahyaee, K. H., Hussain, S. M., & Taylor, G. (2018). Market risk disclosures, corporate governance structure and political connections: Evidence from GCC firms. *Applied Economics Letters, 25*(19), 1346–1350.

Ali, C. B. (2014). Corporate governance, principal-principal agency conflicts, and disclosure. *Journal of Applied Business Research, 30*(2), 419.

Ali, R., Amin, A., Rehman, R. U., & Elamer, A. A. (2025). Gender diversity in boardrooms: The impact of female co-opted directors on corporate governance, firm risk, and firm value. *International Journal of Manpower*. https://doi.org/10.1108/ijm-11-2024-0795

Alsaadi, A. (2024). Signalling through accountability reporting for family firms: Does the institutional environment matter? *Spanish Journal of Finance and Accounting/Revista Española de Financiación y Contabilidad, 53*(1), 75–98.

Alshirah, M. H., Alshira'h, A. F., & Lutfi, A. (2022). Political connection, family ownership and corporate risk disclosure: Empirical evidence from Jordan. *Meditari Accountancy Research, 30*(5), 1241–1264.

Alshirah, M. H., Rahman, A. A., & Mustapa, I. R. (2020). Board of directors' characteristics and corporate risk disclosure: The moderating role of family ownership. *EuroMed Journal of Business, 15*(2), 219–252.

Alshirah, M., & Alshira'h, A. (2024). The impact of corporate ownership structure on corporate risk disclosure: Evidence from an emerging economy. *Competitiveness Review: An International Business Journal, 34*(2), 370–395.

Anderson, R. C., Duru, A., & Reeb, D. M. (2012). Investment policy in family controlled firms. *Journal of Banking & Finance, 36*(6), 1744–1758.

Attig, N., El Ghoul, S., Guedhami, O., & Rizeanu, S. (2013). The governance role of multiple large shareholders: Evidence from the valuation of cash holdings. *Journal of Management & Governance, 17*(2), 419–451.

Baek, H. Y., Cho, D. D., & Fazio, P. L. (2016). Family ownership, control and corporate capital structure: An examination of small capitalization public firms. *Journal of Family Business Management, 6*(2), 169–185.

Baek, J. S., & Kim, J. (2015). Cofounders and the value of family firms. *Emerging Markets Finance and Trade, 51*(Suppl 3), 20–33.

Baig, M. H., Jin, X., & Ali, R. (2024). Politically connected business and real earnings management: The moderating role of family control and audit quality. *Journal of Accounting in Emerging Economies, 14*(5), 970–992.

Berrone, P., Cruz, C., & Gomez-Mejia, L. R. (2012). Socioemotional wealth in family firms: Theoretical dimensions, assessment approaches, and agenda for future research. *Family Business Review, 25*(3), 258–279.

Bona-Sánchez, C., Pérez-Alemán, J., & Santana Martín, D. J. (2020). Political ties and corporate tax burden in Spain. *Spanish Journal of Finance and Accounting/Revista Española de Financiación y Contabilidad, 49*(1), 74–93.

Boubakri, N., & Ghouma, H. (2010). Control/ownership structure, creditor rights protection, and the cost of debt financing: International evidence. *Journal of Banking & Finance, 34*(10), 2481–2499.

Brandt, E., Silva, M. Z. D., & Beck, F. (2021). Influence of family culture on enterprise risk management in Brazilian companies. *Revista de Administração Contemporânea, 25*(06), e190082.

Brogi, M., Gallucci, C., & Santulli, R. (2021). Does one size fit all? A configurational approach to board effectiveness in limiting the excess cash. *Management Decision, 59*(13), 136–163.

Burgstaller, J., & Wagner, E. (2015). How do family ownership and founder management affect capital structure decisions and adjustment of SMEs? Evidence from a bank-based economy. *The Journal of Risk Finance, 16*(1), 73–101.

Cai, Y., Li, M., Guo, S., & Nan, X. (2023). Former CEO director and audit fees. *Emerging Markets Finance and Trade, 59*(4), 1074–1088.

Canbaloglu, B., Alp, O. S., & Gurgun, G. (2022). Debt maturity structure and stock price crash risk: The case of Turkiye. *Borsa Istanbul Review, 22*(5), 985–991.

Cao, F., Li, S., Dai, M., & Li, J. (2023). Your heart is where your treasure is: Family chairman and tax avoidance in family-controlled firms. *Journal of Business Research, 154*, 113298.

Caprio, L., Del Giudice, A., & Signori, A. (2020). Cash holdings in family firms: CEO identity and implications for firm value. *European Financial Management, 26*(2), 386–415.

Chaabouni, I., Ben Mbarek, N., & Ayadi, E. (2025). Do ESG risk scores and board attributes impact corporate performance? Evidence from Saudi-listed companies. *Journal of Risk and Financial Management, 18*(2), 83.

Chakraborty, I. (2018). Effects of ownership structure on capital structure of Indian listed firms: Role of business groups vis-à-vis stand-alone firms. *Emerging Markets Finance and Trade, 54*(10), 2315–2332.

Chen, I. J., & Wang, D. K. (2019). Real option, idiosyncratic risk, and corporate investment: Evidence from Taiwan family firms. *Pacific-Basin Finance Journal, 57*, 101029.

Chen, Y. R., Huang, Y. L., & Chen, C. N. (2009). Financing constraints, ownership control, and cross-border M&As: Evidence from nine East Asian economies. *Corporate Governance: An International Review, 17*(6), 665–680.

Di Giuli, A., Caselli, S., & Gatti, S. (2011). Are small family firms financially sophisticated? *Journal of Banking & Finance, 35*(11), 2931–2944.

Eulaiwi, B., Al-Hadi, A. H. A., Duong, L., Perrin, B., & Taylor, G. (2023). Related party transactions, ownership structures and cost of debt: Evidence from GCC listed firms. *Accounting Research Journal, 36*(4/5), 471–494.

Faghfouri, P., Kraiczy, N. D., Hack, A., & Kellermanns, F. W. (2015). Ready for a crisis? How supervisory boards affect the formalized crisis procedures of small and medium-sized family firms in Germany. *Review of Managerial Science, 9*(2), 317–338.

Ferreira, M. P., Ribeiro, A. M., & Vicente, E. F. R. (2025). The moderating effect of idiosyncratic risk on the market value of cash: A study of Brazilian family and non-family businesses. *Revista Contabilidade & Finanças, 36*(97), e1875.

Gavana, G., Gottardo, P., & Moisello, A. M. (2024). Related party transactions and earnings management in family firms: The moderating role of board characteristics. *Journal of Family Business Management, 14*(1), 171–198.

Gottardo, P., & Moisello, A. M. (2015). The impact of socioemotional wealth on family firms' financial performance. *Problems and Perspectives in Management, 13*(1), 67–77.

Guizani, A., Lakhal, F., & Lakhal, N. (2018). The cash flow sensitivity of cash in family firms: Does the board of directors matter? *Managerial Finance, 44*(11), 1364–1380.

Hagelin, N., Holmén, M., & Pramborg, B. (2006). Family ownership, dual-class shares, and risk management. *Global Finance Journal, 16*(3), 283–301.

Haj-Salem, I., Damak Ayadi, S., & Hussainey, K. (2020). The joint effect of corporate risk disclosure and corporate governance on firm value. *International Journal of Disclosure and Governance, 17*(2), 123–140.

Heaney, R., & Holmen, M. (2008). Family ownership and the cost of under-diversification. *Applied Financial Economics, 18*(21), 1721–1737.

Holmen, M., & Nivorozhkin, E. (2007). The impact of family ownership and dual class shares on takeover risk. *Applied Financial Economics, 17*(10), 785–804.

Huang, H. H., & Chan, M. L. (2013). Long-term stock returns after a substantial increase in the debt ratio. *Applied Financial Economics, 23*(6), 449–460.

Huybrechts, J., Voordeckers, W., & Lybaert, N. (2013). Entrepreneurial risk taking of private family firms: The influence of a nonfamily CEO and the moderating effect of CEO tenure. *Family Business Review, 26*(2), 161–179.

Imperatore, C., & Pope, P. F. (2024). Do tenure-based voting rights help mitigate the family firm control-growth dilemma? *Strategic Management Journal, 45*(11), 2257–2274.

Kallmuenzer, A., & Peters, M. (2018). Entrepreneurial behaviour, firm size and financial performance: The case of rural tourism family firms. *Tourism Recreation Research, 43*(1), 2–14.

Kim, C., Pantzalis, C., & Park, J. C. (2014). Do family owners use firm hedging policy to hedge personal undiversified wealth risk? *Financial Management, 43*(2), 415–444.

Kotey, R. A., Kusi, B., & Akomatey, R. (2019). Ownership structure and profitability of listed firms in an emerging market. *Growing Science. Accounting*, (Online First), 1–16.

Kraus, S., Kallmuenzer, A., Stieger, D., Peters, M., & Calabrò, A. (2018). Entrepreneurial paths to family firm performance. *Journal of Business Research, 88*, 382–387.

Krishnan, G., & Peytcheva, M. (2019). The risk of fraud in family firms: Assessments of external auditors. *Journal of Business Ethics, 157*(1), 261–278.

La Rosa, F., Bernini, F., & Verona, R. (2020). Ownership structure and the cost of equity in the European context: The mediating effect of earnings management. *Meditari Accountancy Research, 28*(3), 485–514.

Lardon, A., Deloof, M., & Jorissen, A. (2017). Outside CEOs, board control and the financing policy of small privately held family firms. *Journal of Family Business Strategy, 8*(1), 29–41.

Lee, E. J., Chae, J., & Lee, Y. K. (2018). Family ownership and risk taking. *Finance Research Letters, 25*, 69–75.

Lee, G., Bae, M., Sohn, J., Han, C., & Cho, J. (2024). Does voluntary environmental information disclosure prevent stock price crash risk?–Comparative analysis of chaebol and non-chaebol in Korea. *Energy economics, 131*, 107394.

Lwango, A., Coeurderoy, R., & Giménez Roche, G. A. (2017). Family influence and SME performance under conditions of firm size and age. *Journal of Small Business and Enterprise Development, 24*(3), 629–648.

Mahto, R. V., & Khanin, D. (2015). Satisfaction with past financial performance, risk taking, and future performance expectations in the family business. *Journal of Small Business Management, 53*(3), 801–818.

Matias Gama, A. P., & Manuel Mendes Galvão, J. (2012). Performance, valuation and capital structure: survey of family firms. *Corporate Governance: The International Journal of Business in Society, 12*(2), 199–214.

McConaughy, D. L., Matthews, C. H., & Fialko, A. S. (2001). Founding family controlled firms: Performance, risk, and value. *Journal of Small Business Management, 39*(1), 31–49.

Mefteh-Wali, S., & Hussain, N. (2024). Do foreign currency risk management strategies increase value in family business? *International Review of Financial Analysis, 93*, 103151.

Miralles-Marcelo, J. L., del Mar Miralles-Quirós, M., & Lisboa, I. (2014). The impact of family control on firm performance: Evidence from Portugal and Spain. *Journal of Family Business Strategy, 5*(2), 156–168.

Oh, H., Park, J., & Kim, B. (2022). Managerial ability and bond rating: A focus on controlling shareholders' ownership structure. *Emerging Markets Finance and Trade, 58*(7), 2093–2107.

Otero-González, L., Rodríguez-Gil, L. I., Vivel-Búa, M., & Tamayo-Herrera, A. (2022). Family ownership, corporate governance and risk-taking. *Journal of Risk and Financial Management, 15*(3), 110.

Parrado-Martínez, P., Comino-Jurado, M., & Sánchez-Andújar, S. (2024). Cash holdings decision-making in Spanish family firms: Exploring the impact of heterogeneity. *Managerial and Decision Economics, 45*(6), 3761–3774.

Peláez-León, J. D., & Sanchez-Marin, G. (2022). Socioemotional wealth and human resource policies: Effects on family firm performance. *International Journal of Entrepreneurial Behavior & Research, 28*(1), 109–135.

Peruzzi, V. (2024). In family we trust: Religiosity and credit rationing in family-owned firms. *Economics Letters, 243*, 111953.

Poletti-Hughes, J., & Briano-Turrent, G. C. (2019). Gender diversity on the board of directors and corporate risk: A behavioural agency theory perspective. *International Review of Financial Analysis, 62*, 80–90.

Poletti-Hughes, J., & Williams, J. (2019). The effect of family control on value and risk-taking in Mexico: A socioemotional wealth approach. *International Review of Financial Analysis, 63*, 369–381.

Rajverma, A. K., Misra, A. K., Mohapatra, S., & Chandra, A. (2019). Impact of ownership structure and dividend on firm performance and firm risk. *Managerial Finance, 45*(8), 1041–1061.

Rasheed, M. S., Kouser, S., & Ling, Z. (2025). Corporate governance and stock price crash risk: Insights from an emerging market. *Asia-Pacific Financial Markets, 32*(2), 691–709.

Roffia, P., Simón-Moya, V., & Sendra García, J. (2022). Board of director attributes: Effects on financial performance in SMEs. *International Entrepreneurship and Management Journal, 18*(3), 1141–1172.

Roger, P., & Schatt, A. (2016). Idiosyncratic risk, private benefits, and the value of family firms. *Finance Research Letters, 17*, 235–245.

Rodríguez, Y. E., Gómez, J. M., Chávez, H., & Chea, J. (2021). Family business risk-taking and financial performance: Is it easier said than done? *Journal of Family Business Strategy, 12*(4), 100435.

Saghi-Zedek, N., & Tarazi, A. (2015). Excess control rights, financial crisis and bank profitability and risk. *Journal of Banking & Finance, 55*, 361–379.

Salem, I. H., Ayadi, S. D., & Hussainey, K. (2019). Corporate governance and risk disclosure quality: Tunisian evidence. *Journal of Accounting in Emerging Economies, 9*(4), 567–602.

Shahzad, A., Nazir, M. S., Morais, F., & Asghar Butt, A. (2025). Ownership structure, board composition and CEO dominance: What does really matters to corporate deleveraging policies? *Corporate Governance: The International Journal of Business in Society, 25*(4), 786–814.

Shandiz, M. T., Zadeh, F. N., & Askarany, D. (2022). The interactive effect of ownership structure on the relationship between annual board report readability and stock price crash risk. *Journal of Risk and Financial Management, 15*(6), 268.

Srinidhi, B., & Liao, Q. (2020). Family firms and crash risk: Alignment and entrenchment effects. *Journal of Contemporary Accounting & Economics, 16*(2), 100204.

Tran, O. T. K., Nguyen, A. H. V., Nguyen, P. Y. N., & Duong, K. D. (2023). CEO overpower and stock price crash risk: Evidence from family businesses in Vietnam. *Journal of Eastern European and Central Asian Research (JEECAR), 10*(3), 425–438.

Watkins-Fassler, K., Briano-Turrent, G. D. C., & Rodríguez-Ariza, L. (2019). Performance and abilities of family-member CEOS in a context of formal institutional weakness. *El trimestre económico, 86*(341), 179–219.

Wu, S. F., Fang, C. Y., & Chen, W. (2020). Corporate governance and stock price crash risk: Evidence from Taiwan. *Managerial and Decision Economics, 41*(7), 1312–1326.

# Chapter 5
# Innovation, Digitalization, and Risk in Family Businesses

**Abstract** This chapter analyzes the intersection of entrepreneurship, innovation, digitalization, and risk in family businesses, focusing on the bibliometric cluster "Entrepreneurship, innovation, digitalization, and risk" (yellow cluster). The analysis shows that, compared to their non-family counterparts, family businesses tend to adopt a more cautious entrepreneurial approach, favoring incremental innovations, reactive strategies, and gradual change processes aimed at limiting risk exposure and preserving the continuity of family control. At the same time, the chapter highlights how the presence of a new generation of leadership, the contribution of external human capital, and the formalization of governance processes can trigger trajectories of transformation in which innovation, including digital innovation, becomes a lever for reducing perceived risk, strengthening competitiveness, and opening the entrepreneurial family to more systematic risk management approaches.

**Keywords** Innovation · Digital transformation · Entrepreneurial orientation · Risk-taking · Incremental innovation · Generational change · Risk

## 5.1 Entrepreneurial Orientation and Family Business Risk

Entrepreneurial orientation (EO), understood as the combination of innovativeness, proactivity, and risk-taking, is a fundamental lever for the development of family businesses. However, its impact is deeply influenced by the nature of the family itself and its role within the organization. Several studies show that high family involvement in management tends to reduce the innovation and risk-taking components of EO, generating a more conservative entrepreneurial orientation. Casillas and Moreno (2010) highlight that, although EO is positively correlated with growth, this relationship weakens when the family exercises substantial control over operational management. In line with these results, Campopiano et al. (2020) show that the presence of family members in top management can mitigate the positive impact of EO on growth, while more balanced configurations, with passive family



A. M. Moisello, P. Gottardo, *Risk and Sustainability in Family Businesses*, SpringerBriefs in Finance, https://doi.org/10.1007/978-3-032-19995-9_5

shareholders or shareholders belonging to different generations, can instead foster greater entrepreneurial openness, if there is strategic consistency.

Craig et al. (2014) demonstrate that proactivity is the dimension with the most significant effect on innovation in family businesses, while risk propensity has a more limited impact than in non-family businesses, due to the desire to preserve control and socioemotional wealth (SEW). This behavior is confirmed by Lasio et al. (2024), who suggest that EO in Italian family businesses is more oriented toward conservation than transformation, particularly in the presence of strong family ties. Casillas et al. (2011) further explore this issue, observing that EO and performance are positively correlated only when companies have adequate organizational capabilities.

Ferrari et al. (2024) demonstrate that a clan-based, centralized environment can support consistent EO only in single-generation contexts. In contrast, the presence of multiple generations can lead to strategic divergences and latent conflicts that limit the propensity to take risks. Confirmation is provided by Mucci et al. (2022), who analyze the effect of SEW on the three dimensions of EO, highlighting that subsequent generations exhibit a greater propensity to take risks, whereas founders tend to favor defensive proactivity. Furthermore, Garcia-Piqueres et al. (2019) highlight that sharing leadership between family and non-family members promotes a better balance between innovation and risk control.

Sciascia et al. (2015) demonstrate that an excessively high level of EO can compromise the survival of family businesses due to excessive risk exposure. Similarly, Kallmuenzer et al. (2018) emphasize that proactivity and autonomy improve financial performance only if balanced by effective internal control mechanisms and a clear value hierarchy. The synergy between EO and dynamic capabilities appears particularly relevant, as it enables companies to adapt to environmental changes and capitalize on business opportunities (Letonja et al., 2016; Lopez-Fernandez et al., 2016). In this sense, Li et al. (2021) emphasize the role of intra-family trust in strengthening EO, facilitating innovative choices even in risky contexts.

The literature has also highlighted that succession and leadership dynamics strongly influence entrepreneurial propensity, showing that successors with international training and a global strategic vision tend to increase EO, mainly if supported by an effective transfer of power from the previous generation (Zhu & Kang, 2022). A similar orientation emerges from Naldi et al. (2007), who find weaker EO in family businesses than in non-family businesses and report that this gap can be reduced by introducing external managers or younger members into leadership roles. Empirical evidence indicates that the influence of the institutional context is equally significant, as differences in regulatory and cultural regimes shape risk-taking propensity, especially in the early stages of entrepreneurial ventures (Stenholm et al., 2016; Yu, 2023). Finally, Zhiyong et al. (2024) highlight that Chinese family-owned manufacturing SMEs have lower EO than non-family-owned SMEs, but that this orientation increases significantly in the presence of external human capital and formal governance structures.

## 5.2 Risk Propensity and Innovation Strategies

An inherent tension exists between the desire for continuity and the drive for change, characterizing the relationship between risk-taking and innovation in family businesses. The conservative orientation typical of family businesses, linked to the desire to preserve socioemotional capital (SEW), tends to hinder the adoption of radical innovations, which are perceived as highly risky and potentially destabilizing (Block, 2012; Hu & Hughes, 2020). This brake on innovation is reinforced by structural constraints, such as a preference for self-financing and limited access to credit, especially in small businesses (Minetti et al., 2015). However, in turbulent or highly competitive contexts, family businesses can respond by adopting 'reactive risk taking', in which innovation serves as a means of defense and survival (Cucculelli & Peruzzi, 2020).

Many studies highlight that the nature of innovation pursued by family businesses is predominantly incremental, making it more easily compatible with the desire to maintain stability (Chung et al., 2021; Zhiyong et al., 2024). Radical innovation, on the other hand, often requires a break with established routines and an acceptance of greater uncertainty, which entrepreneurial families are reluctant to embrace unless specific disruptive events occur, such as a performance crisis or generational succession (Hu & Hughes, 2020; Zhu & Kang, 2022). Not surprisingly, the involvement of young family managers or CEOs with international training appears to be an enabling factor for greater openness to risky innovation (Chung et al., 2021; Zhu & Kang, 2022).

The institutional context plays a significant moderating role. De Massis et al. (2018) demonstrate, in the Chinese context, that family businesses, despite operating in an institutionally fragile environment, invest in R&D to strengthen their position and ensure transgenerational continuity. Similarly, Yin et al. (2023) observe that family legacy can act as a brake if not accompanied by an adequate risk culture. In contrast, employment stability and trust among top management favor the adoption of even riskier innovations.

Family governance has a decisive influence on the relationship between innovation and risk. Family businesses with formal governance, a performance orientation, and non-family CEOs show a greater propensity to innovate, even in uncertain conditions (Martinez-Bobillo et al., 2021). Cognitive and generational diversity is another key element: Kraiczy et al. (2015) show that it stimulates product innovation and mitigates risk perception, although excessive fragmentation can slow down decision-making.

Some authors emphasize the combination of entrepreneurial culture and environmental context. Aloulou (2018) proposes an integrated view, according to which the interaction between proactivity and risk taking generates incremental innovation in the presence of stable family control. Liu et al. (2025) confirm that the ability to promote organizational autonomy and reduce structural rigidity is crucial for unlocking the latent innovation potential in family businesses. Furthermore, open innovation strategies are more frequently adopted by risk-prone firms, facilitating radical innovation (Kim et al., 2023).

At the cultural and value levels, risk propensity is strengthened when family values emphasize learning, flexibility, and social legitimacy. Ng et al. (2022) show that these values stimulate investment in R&D and innovative performance. The adoption of corporate social responsibility (CSR) practices can serve as a mechanism to legitimize and mitigate perceived risk, thereby facilitating the introduction of sustainable innovations (Vollero et al., 2019). Finally, Gundry et al. (2014) offer a gender perspective, showing that family businesses led by women tend to manage risk collectively and creatively, with positive effects on adaptive innovation.

In summary, the relationship between risk-taking and innovation in family businesses is far from straightforward; it depends on the life-cycle stage, generational composition, governance structure, internal trust mechanisms, and external pressures. When properly balanced, risk appetite can be transformed from an inhibiting factor to a catalyst for innovation, especially in the presence of open leadership, substantial social capital, and a shared entrepreneurial orientation.

## 5.3 Risk Taking and Proactivity

Although both dimensions are central components of entrepreneurial orientation, they manifest themselves differently in family-controlled businesses, where organizational culture, governance, and the generation in charge play a decisive role. As Ceipek et al. (2021) note, family organizational culture tends to favor stability and risk aversion, thereby mitigating the natural association between proactive behavior and risk-taking. However, when perceived opportunities align with the family's founding values, such as sustainable growth or generational continuity, the firm may accept controlled levels of risk to support proactive initiatives.

The presence of formal governance and well-structured control mechanisms promotes a balance between entrepreneurial boldness and strategic foresight (Chakrabarti & Mondal, 2020), while organizational culture plays a differentiating role. Ferrari et al. (2024) note that 'clan-like' organizational environments promote proactivity, while more hierarchical contexts are more conducive to risk-taking. Proactivity can therefore act as a mitigating lever for family risk, allowing changes to be anticipated with less exposed strategies, as shown by Chung et al. (2021) and Hernández-Linares et al. (2020). As highlighted by Kallmuenzer et al. (2018), family businesses can exhibit high proactivity even in the presence of low-risk propensity, particularly when supported by an effective agency structure and well-defined socioemotional objectives.

Generational dynamics further influence this balance, and evidence suggests that the second generation tends to exhibit greater openness to both risk and proactivity, particularly when the family culture is change-oriented (Gutuleac et al., 2025). Kraus et al. (2012) reinforce this idea, noting that family businesses operate between cultural and institutional constraints that favor proactivity for reputational reasons but limit risk exposure to preserve control. Liu et al. (2025) observe that companies founded and led by first-generation entrepreneurs balance risk and proactivity differently than those led by successors, who tend to adopt more open strategies. In situations of intense competitive pressure, even companies with a low-risk appetite adopt proactive branding strategies (Kuang et al., 2024).

From environmental and institutional perspectives, organizational culture influences family businesses' ability to anticipate market changes, and family reputational capital can encourage more daring risk-taking decisions (Min, 2021). Consistent with this, Mirza et al. (2024) demonstrate that family businesses in emerging countries venture into international markets with proactive strategies only if they possess sufficient relational capital to absorb the associated risks. This finding aligns with Patel and Chrisman's (2014) observation that family culture must be able to sustain a certain degree of risk for strategic proactivity to translate into superior performance.

The ability to anticipate and respond to external shocks translates into greater resilience, as illustrated by Revilla et al. (2016), who demonstrate a link between decision-making flexibility, family cohesion, and more effective risk absorption. In internationalization strategy, proactivity also manifests itself through gradual approaches aimed at limiting exposure to excessive risks (Werner et al., 2018). Sultan et al. (2024) introduce the role of HRM practices, demonstrating that more flexible leadership models promote entrepreneurial behavior, even in highly uncertain environments.

From the perspective of succession and generational renewal, Zhu and Kang (2022) find that proactivity increases when the successor possesses digital skills and a future-oriented vision. However, this may clash with traditional family values that favor internal cohesion. Similarly, Zhiyong et al. (2024) show that strategic proactivity is often a selective response to competitive or regulatory pressures, constrained by the balance between family and economic objectives.

## 5.4 Digital Transformation and Risk-Taking

The adoption of digital technologies, while offering significant competitive advantages, is often hindered by perceptions of technological risk and concerns about the loss of identity and control. As Bornhausen and Wulf (2024) observe, digital risk aversion is more pronounced among families with strong intentions to maintain transgenerational control. In contrast, the presence of external managers and a less obsessive focus on generational transition favors greater openness to innovation.

New-generation leadership plays a crucial role in mitigating the perception of risk associated with digitalization, as successors who are more digitally competent and less tied to established routines tend to view digital transformation as a strategic opportunity (Arz, 2021; Li et al., 2021). Kim et al. (2023) introduce the concept of digital champions, that is, young family members who promote digital innovation and mitigate internal resistance through narratives compatible with family values.

Digitalization is also a robust risk-management tool, capable of reducing operational and environmental uncertainty while stimulating more aggressive investment in innovation (Chen et al., 2024). However, for this to occur, it is necessary to overcome the decision-making conflicts typical of family governance, and a shift from causal decision-making logic to effectuation paradigms can help family businesses address uncertainty in a more entrepreneurial manner (Brenk et al., 2019).

Giacomarra et al. (2021) highlight that digital adoption is often hindered by a high perceived risk, but that it can be incorporated into the family regeneration strategy, particularly when supported by identity narratives. In this context, Xu et al. (2024) observe that direct family management can be a hindrance. However, the development of dynamic capabilities and the involvement of the new generation favor a more harmonious change.

From a governance perspective, Yang et al. (2025) and Zhu and Kang (2022) demonstrate that integrating formal governance tools and defining clear digital strategies enable family businesses to overcome their aversion to innovation, thereby making digital risk more manageable. Oke et al. (2025) emphasize that digital transformation is not just a technological issue but requires a new entrepreneurial vision, supported by a structure that legitimizes risk-taking.

Ultimately, interaction with external stakeholders is a crucial catalyst for digitalization. Zhiyong et al. (2024) demonstrate that partnerships with technology providers and external consultants help family businesses bridge the digital gap by facilitating the integration of tradition and innovation.

## 5.5 Discussion: Tensions Between Innovation, Risk, and Entrepreneurial Orientation

Risk management in family businesses, based on evidence from the analysis of Entrepreneurial Orientation, presents a set of structural strengths and weaknesses that stem from the interplay of cultural, organizational, and intergenerational factors.

A key strength lies in the proactivity exhibited by many family businesses, particularly when this is aligned with deeply rooted values such as continuity, reputation, and long-term sustainability (Craig et al., 2014; Ceipek et al., 2021). This proactive orientation enables them to anticipate environmental changes through strategies that are relatively low-risk yet effective. In this sense, second-generation leadership, which is more open to innovation and digital transformation, can increase risk appetite, facilitating the evolution of the business model (Zhu & Kang, 2022; Gutuleac et al., 2025). This suggests the importance of family businesses investing in training and mentoring programs for younger generations to foster generational change that can drive strategic transformations without compromising family identity.

A second strength is cultural flexibility in dynamic contexts. With open governance, the coexistence of multiple generations, and mixed family-non-family leadership, family businesses can balance boldness and prudence, transforming risk into a lever for innovation and sustainable growth (Garcia-Piqueres et al., 2019; Campopiano et al., 2020). Furthermore, intrafamily trust and internal relational orientation are strategic resources for managing uncertainty, thereby providing stability and cohesion in decision-making processes (Li et al., 2021). Companies should value and systematize these resources through shared governance tools and strategic communication to transform trust into organizational capital.

Finally, the ability to integrate formal governance tools and adopt a digital transformation guided by vision and strategic skills emerges as a further strength in more advanced companies. Technology is increasingly perceived not as a threat but to reduce operational risk and strengthen competitiveness, particularly in the presence of internal digital champions and alliances with external stakeholders (Bornhausen & Wulf, 2024; Kim et al., 2023; Zhiyong et al., 2024).

However, the approach to risk in family businesses presents numerous challenges. First, risk aversion, often stemming from a desire to preserve socioemotionalwealth (SEW) and intergenerational control, tends to curb the most dynamic components of EO, such as innovation and risk-taking (Craig et al., 2014). This conservative orientation can lead to underperformance, particularly in competitive environments or during periods of environmental turbulence. Family businesses should therefore develop strategic assessment tools that enable them to distinguish between operational and identity risks, thereby creating space for innovation without compromising continuity.

Second, many family businesses operate with limited organizational capabilities; in the absence of adequate resources, EO risks becoming a source of strategic frustration (Casillas et al., 2011). A preference for self-financing, combined with limited access to credit, compromises the ability to invest in high-risk innovation (Minetti et al., 2015). Furthermore, overly centralized or founder-dominated management structures can reduce the ability to take bold decisions, even when conditions require it (Mucci et al., 2022). Companies should consider introducing strategic finance and participatory governance tools to support more ambitious resource management.

A third weakness concerns the management of digitalization. Although digital transformation is recognized as necessary, it is often hampered by cultural resistance, fear of change, and a lack of shared vision. Digital innovation is adopted only if it is compatible with family culture, which slows its diffusion and reduces its potential impact, particularly in family-run SMEs (Giacomarra et al., 2021; Xu et al., 2024).

Finally, the absence of strategic integration between EO and dynamic capabilities can compromise the response to external shocks. Entrepreneurial orientation improves performance only when accompanied by organizational flexibility, openness to learning, and efficient coordination mechanisms (Letonja et al., 2016; Lopez-Fernandez et al., 2016). Otherwise, risk becomes an unmanaged threat rather than an opportunity for growth.

This implies that digital transformation can become a lever for strategic regeneration and uncertainty reduction, but only if accompanied by targeted interventions. Among these, the inclusion of non-family managers or the promotion of internal digital champions are practical tools for overcoming cultural barriers to innovation and mitigating perceived risk (Kim et al., 2023; Arz, 2021). At the same time, the formal structuring of governance and investment in generational training are enabling factors for addressing the complexity of digitalization (Xu et al., 2024; Yang et al., 2025). Finally, alliances with external stakeholders are proving useful in bridging the gap between tradition and innovation, acting as a bridge between the needs for protection and transformation (Zhiyong et al., 2024).

## References

Aloulou, W. J. (2018). Examining entrepreneurial orientation's dimensions–performance relationship in Saudi family businesses: Contingency role of family involvement in management. *Journal of Family Business Management, 8*(2), 126–145.

Arz, C. (2021). From family commitment to entrepreneurial orientation: Exploring the role of cultural mechanisms in mature family firms. *International Studies of Management & Organization, 51*(4), 297–327.

Block, J. H. (2012). R&D investments in family and founder firms: An agency perspective. *Journal of Business Venturing, 27*(2), 248–265.

Bornhausen, A. M., & Wulf, T. (2024). Digital innovation in family firms: The roles of non-family managers and transgenerational control intentions. *Small Business Economics, 62*(4), 1429–1448.

Brenk, S., Lüttgens, D., Diener, K., & Piller, F. (2019). Learning from failures in business model innovation: Solving decision-making logic conflicts through intrapreneurial effectuation. *Journal of Business Economics, 89*(8), 1097–1147.

Campopiano, G., Brumana, M., Minola, T., & Cassia, L. (2020). Does growth represent chimera or bellerophon for a family business? The role of entrepreneurial orientation and family influence nuances. *European Management Review, 17*(3), 765–783.

Casillas, J. C., & Moreno, A. M. (2010). The relationship between entrepreneurial orientation and growth: The moderating role of family involvement. *Entrepreneurship & Regional Development, 22*(3–4), 265–291.

Casillas, J. C., Moreno, A. M., & Barbero, J. L. (2011). Entrepreneurial orientation of family firms: Family and environmental dimensions. *Journal of Family Business Strategy, 2*(2), 90–100.

Ceipek, R., Hautz, J., De Massis, A., Matzler, K., & Ardito, L. (2021). Digital transformation through exploratory and exploitative internet of things innovations: The impact of family management and technological diversification. *Journal of Product Innovation Management, 38*(1), 142–165.

Chakrabarti, A. B., & Mondal, A. (2020). The effect of institutional transition on entrepreneurial orientation of family businesses: Evidence from India. *International Journal of Entrepreneurial Behavior & Research, 26*(1), 76–97.

Chen, S., Li, Z., Chu, L., & Cao, Q. (2024). Excess control of family board seats and corporate innovation. *Journal of Business Finance & Accounting, 51*(9–10), 2635–2667.

Chung, P. H., Lee, C. J., Wu, H. L., & Lee, C. Y. (2021). Innovation promoter or inhibitor? Non-family CEO's effect on innovation in family businesses. *IEEE Transactions on Engineering Management, 70*(9), 3143–3155.

Craig, J. B., Pohjola, M., Kraus, S., & Jensen, S. H. (2014). Exploring relationships among proactiveness, risk-taking and innovation output in family and non-family firms. *Creativity and Innovation Management, 23*(2), 199–210.

Cucculelli, M., & Peruzzi, V. (2020). Post-crisis firm survival, business model changes, and learning: Evidence from the Italian manufacturing industry. *Small Business Economics, 54*(2), 459–474.

De Massis, A., Ding, S., Kotlar, J., & Wu, Z. (2018). Family involvement and R&D expenses in the context of weak property rights protection: An examination of non-state-owned listed companies in China. *The European Journal of Finance, 24*(16), 1506–1527.

Ferrari, A., Mucci, D. M., & Beck, F. (2024). Organizational culture, generational involvement and entrepreneurial orientation components: A replication study. *Journal of Entrepreneurship in Emerging Economies, 16*(4), 868–890.

García-Piqueres, G., Serrano-Bedia, A. M., & Pérez-Pérez, M. (2019). Knowledge management practices and innovation outcomes: The moderating role of risk-taking and proactiveness. *Administrative Sciences, 9*(4), 75.

Giacomarra, M., Shams, S. R., Crescimanno, M., Sakka, G., Gregori, G. L., & Galati, A. (2021). Internal vs. external R&D teams: Evidences from the Italian wine industry. *Journal of Business Research, 128*, 752–761.

Gundry, L. K., Kickul, J. R., Iakovleva, T., & Carsrud, A. L. (2014). Women-owned family businesses in transitional economies: Key influences on firm innovativeness and sustainability. *Journal of Innovation and Entrepreneurship, 3*(1), 8.

Gutuleac, R., Giachino, C., Vilamová, Š., & Ferraris, A. (2025). Demystifying sustainable innovation and governance in family firms: A critical review. *Technological Forecasting and Social Change, 212*, 123994.

Hernández-Linares, R., Kellermanns, F. W., López-Fernández, M. C., & Sarkar, S. (2020). The effect of socioemotional wealth on the relationship between entrepreneurial orientation and family business performance. *BRQ Business Research Quarterly, 23*(3), 174–192.

Hu, Q., & Hughes, M. (2020). Radical innovation in family firms: A systematic analysis and research agenda. *International Journal of Entrepreneurial Behavior & Research, 26*(6), 1199–1234.

Kallmuenzer, A., Strobl, A., & Peters, M. (2018). Tweaking the entrepreneurial orientation–performance relationship in family firms: The effect of control mechanisms and family-related goals. *Review of Managerial Science, 12*(4), 855–883.

Kim, T., Sexton, J. C., & Marler, L. E. (2023). Innovation as a mixed gamble in family firms: The moderating effect of inter-organizational cooperation. *Small Business Economics, 60*(4), 1389–1408.

Kraiczy, N. D., Hack, A., & Kellermanns, F. W. (2015). What makes a family firm innovative? CEO risk-taking propensity and the organizational context of family firms. *Journal of Product Innovation Management, 32*(3), 334–348.

Kraus, S., Pohjola, M., & Koponen, A. (2012). Innovation in family firms: An empirical analysis linking organizational and managerial innovation to corporate success. *Review of Managerial Science, 6*(3), 265–286.

Kuang, X. W., Luo, C. Y., & Xu, J. M. (2024). "Spousal cogovernance" and enterprise innovation: An empirical study based on China's listed family businesses. *Applied Economics, 56*(57), 7807–7824.

Lasio, V., Gómez, J. M., Rosso, J., & Sánchez, A. (2024). Entrepreneurial orientation and socioemotional wealth as enablers of the impact of digital transformation in family firms. *Journal of Family Business Management, 14*(6), 1268–1294.

Letonja, M., Jeraj, M., & Maric, M. (2016). An empirical study of the relationship between entrepreneurial competences and innovativeness of successors in family SMEs. *Organizacija, 49*(4), 225.

Li, W. H., Luo, J. H., De Sisto, M., & Bartram, T. (2021). Born to rebel? The owner birth order and R&D investments in Chinese family firms. *Journal of Product Innovation Management, 38*(4), 421–446.

Liu, Y., Zhang, S., Chen, F., & Mu, Y. (2025). Clan culture and digital transformation: Evidence from Chinese family firms. *Accounting & Finance, 65*(1), 971–1008.

Lopez-Fernandez, M. C., Serrano-Bedia, A. M., & Gómez-López, R. (2016). Determinants of innovation decision in small and medium-sized family enterprises. *Journal of Small Business and Enterprise Development, 23*(2), 408–427.

Martínez Bobillo, A., Rodríguez Sanz, J. A., & Tejerina Gaite, F. (2021). Explanatory and predictive drivers of entrepreneurial orientation and innovation capacity: Evidence from family enterprises. *Cuadernos de Gestión, 21*(2).

Min, B. S. (2021). Heterogeneity of R&D in family firms. *Journal of Business Research, 129*, 88–95.

Minetti, R., Murro, P., & Paiella, M. (2015). Ownership structure, governance, and innovation. *European Economic Review, 80*, 165–193.

Mirza, S. S., Ahsan, T., Al-Gamrh, B., Majeed, M. A., & Muhammad, F. (2024). The impact of economic policy uncertainty on corporate innovation in China: the role of family ownership and political connections. *Applied Economics, 56*(59), 8586–8605.

Mucci, D. M., Beck, F., & Ferrari, A. (2022). Socioemotional wealth and entrepreneurial orientation in different family businesses' generational stages. *BAR-Brazilian Administration Review, 19*(02), e210053.

Naldi, L., Nordqvist, M., Sjöberg, K., & Wiklund, J. (2007). Entrepreneurial orientation, risk taking, and performance in family firms. *Family Business Review, 20*(1), 33–47.

Ng, P. Y., Dayan, M., & Makri, M. (2022). Influence of socioemotional wealth on non-family managers' risk taking and product innovation in family businesses. *Cross Cultural & Strategic Management, 29*(2), 297–319.

Oke, A., Turla, M., Osobajo, O., & Koutsoukos, S. (2025). Resolving the paradox of green innovation across generations in family firms: An exploratory analysis of incumbents and successors perceptions. *Journal of Family Business Management.* https://doi.org/10.1108/JFBM-03-2025-0068

Patel, P. C., & Chrisman, J. J. (2014). Risk abatement as a strategy for R&D investments in family firms. *Strategic Management Journal, 35*(4), 617–627.

Revilla, A. J., Perez-Luno, A., & Nieto, M. J. (2016). Does family involvement in management reduce the risk of business failure? The moderating role of entrepreneurial orientation. *Family Business Review, 29*(4), 365–379.

Sciascia, S., Nordqvist, M., Mazzola, P., & De Massis, A. (2015). Family ownership and R&D intensity in small-and medium-sized firms. *Journal of Product Innovation Management, 32*(3), 349–360.

Stenholm, P., Pukkinen, T., & Heinonen, J. (2016). Firm growth in family businesses—The role of entrepreneurial orientation and the entrepreneurial activity. *Journal of Small Business Management, 54*(2), 697–713.

Sultan, S., Hudson, M., Habash, N., Sultan, W. I., & Izhiman, N. (2024). Entrepreneurial orientation and Palestinian family-owned businesses: Does governance or geographic location make a difference? *Journal of Small Business and Enterprise Development, 31*(2), 252–271.

Vollero, A., Siano, A., & Della Volpe, M. (2019). A systems perspective for conceptualizing sustainability in long-lived family businesses. Research proposals on risk taking and innovativeness. *Systems Research and Behavioral Science, 36*(1), 111–127.

Werner, A., Schröder, C., & Chlosta, S. (2018). Driving factors of innovation in family and non-family SMEs. *Small Business Economics, 50*(1), 201–218.

Xu, L., Zheng, Y., & Yin, X. (2024). Second-generation involvement and the digitalisation of family firms: Evidence from China. *Technology Analysis & Strategic Management*, 1–16.

Yang, Z., Wu, S., & Huang, Z. (2025). Breaking traditions: An investigation of innovation and risk-taking among copreneurships post-IPO. *European Journal of Innovation Management.*

Yin, Y., Crowley, F., Doran, J., Du, J., & O'Connor, M. (2023). Research and innovation and the role of competition in family owned and managed firms. *International Journal of Entrepreneurial Behavior & Research, 29*(1), 166–194.

Yu, J. (2023). Financial products and family business innovation strategy. *Entrepreneurship Research Journal, 13*(3), 665–691.

Zhiyong, Z., Buyun, X., & Yongbin, X. (2024). Family business financialization and green innovation in China from 2008 to 2023. *International Entrepreneurship and Management Journal, 20*(4), 2453–2479.

Zhu, Z., & Kang, Y. (2022). A far-reaching parental love? Co-governance of intergenerational succession and innovation activities in Chinese family firms. *Management and Organization Review, 18*(2), 358–394.

# Chapter 6
# Internationalization and Global Risk in Family Businesses

**Abstract** This chapter examines the relationship between internationalization and risk management in family businesses, drawing on the bibliometric cluster "Internationalization and global risk." The analysis focuses on how to enter foreign markets, currency risk management, and exposure to institutional and competitive risks in a global context. The results show that family businesses' decisions to internationalize are often guided by conservative logic, oriented toward protecting socio-emotional wealth (SEW) and the stability of family control. These choices are deeply influenced by the generation in charge, the composition of governance bodies, and the institutional characteristics of the destination countries. The chapter also highlights that openness to professionalization, investment in relational capital, and the adoption of advanced risk management tools enable the overcoming of cultural rigidity and risk aversion, thereby favoring more ambitious and resilient international growth strategies.

**Keywords** Internationalization · Global risk · Entry strategies · Institutional risk · Currency/financial risk

## 6.1 Entry Strategy, Internationalization Methods, and Risk

The literature on the entry and internationalization strategy of family businesses reveals a strong link between expansion methods and risk management, highlighting how the family structure profoundly influences strategic choices. In particular, the risk aversion typical of family businesses translates into a preference for less financially and managerially demanding entry modes, such as franchising or greenfield investments, which allow them to maintain control and avoid excessive exposure in uncertain institutional contexts (Andreu et al., 2020; Boellis et al., 2016; D'Allura et al., 2024). This cautious behavior is amplified when there is strong family involvement in ownership and management. At the same time, it tends to decrease in the presence of more professional management or non-family leadership (Monreal-Pérez & Sánchez-Marín, 2017).



A. M. Moisello, P. Gottardo, *Risk and Sustainability in Family Businesses*, SpringerBriefs in Finance, https://doi.org/10.1007/978-3-032-19995-9_6

Another distinguishing factor is the generation in charge: while founders prefer conservative and indirect internationalization strategies, second-generation entrepreneurs exhibit greater openness to riskier yet more ambitious approaches, such as acquisitions or entry into culturally distant markets (Fang et al., 2018; Petrù et al., 2019). Generational diversity can thus act as a lever for greater risk-taking, especially when accompanied by international training experiences or a long-term strategic vision.

Entry mode choices are also strongly influenced by the external environment. Indian family businesses, for example, adopt different strategies depending on the destination: acquisitions in developed countries or greenfield investments in emerging markets, demonstrating a situational approach to risk management (Rienda et al., 2019). In other cases, companies opt for equity alliances, such as joint ventures, to mitigate relational risks with foreign partners, especially when they have substantial experiential capital or operate in highly competitive sectors (Chakraborty & Singla, 2025).

From an operational perspective, family businesses pay particular attention to protecting the family reputation, basing their supply and partnership choices on relational and sustainable criteria rather than purely economic ones (Hasenau & Dutzi, 2023). However, the literature also highlights a reluctance to adopt structured Enterprise Risk Management systems, particularly when the CEO is a family member, as greater internal trust and a lower need for formalization are assumed (Hiebl et al., 2019). Paradoxically, caution is favored in strategic decisions, whereas the formalization of risk management is often underestimated.

Finally, the adoption of imitative behavior, particularly outcome-based imitation, emerges as a mechanism for learning and reducing uncertainty, enabling family businesses to avoid impulsive decisions and prolong their presence in foreign markets (Mazzelli et al., 2023).

## 6.2 Family Control and Currency Risk in Internationalization

Several studies show that, given the same tools available, family businesses do not necessarily stand out for their more frequent use of currency risk hedging instruments compared to non-family companies; however, when they do use them, they do so with a greater speculative bias, influenced by the optimism and overconfidence typical of founders (Aabo et al., 2011). This suggests a paradox: despite a generally cautious attitude, there are cases in which excessive family control leads to unsystematic, risky behavior. A more common strategic alternative is to limit currency exposure at source by reducing penetration in foreign markets or by selecting reference currencies more cautiously, in line with efforts to preserve socioemotional wealth (Anderson et al., 2023).

The degree of family control has non-linear effects on international strategy. Chen et al. (2022) highlight a U-shaped relationship between family control and acquisition size: at intermediate levels, the family reduces investment size to avoid losing control; at high levels, the security of control encourages more ambitious transactions. Similarly, Saurabh and Kumar (2025) demonstrate that descendant family CEOs tend to prefer smaller acquisitions than founders or external managers, highlighting greater risk aversion that independent directors can mitigate. Family governance, therefore, plays a crucial role in managing currency exposure and international risk, not only in operational choices but also in how risk is perceived and internalized (Sahin et al., 2015).

Friction between family and non-family managers can hinder strategic decisions involving high currency exposure; however, effective collaboration can reduce risk perception and promote foreign expansion (De Groote et al., 2023). However, reluctance to adopt structured Enterprise Risk Management tools (Hiebl et al., 2019) risks exposing companies to latent vulnerabilities, especially in complex currency environments.

The perception of international risk is also influenced by the degree of foreign engagement and the generation in charge: first-generation firms are generally more optimistic, whereas greater international engagement increases perceived risk (Claver et al., 2008). Lohe et al. (2021) use the concept of "mixed gamble," that is, the tension between financial risk and socioemotional risk, which can lead firms to prefer conservative strategies even when attractive opportunities are available. Finally, currency risk management is often relationally oriented, as companies prioritize long-term relationships, sustainability criteria, and reputation in their supply choices over standard economic assessments (Hasenau & Dutzi, 2023).

## 6.3 Innovation, Competitiveness in Foreign Markets, and Risk

The propensity to innovate is a key factor supporting internationalization, as highlighted by Braga et al. (2017), who note that the most innovative family businesses are also more inclined to assume the risks associated with entering foreign markets. However, structural risk aversion can limit these strategies, especially when operations are far removed from the core business. In highly competitive environments, innovation serves as a defensive and relaunch mechanism, as competitive pressure prompts family businesses to take greater risks, with risk management mediating the relationship between aggressiveness and strategic prudence (Ali et al., 2024).

According to Chatterjee et al. (2023), digitization and the creation of international networks mitigate the risks associated with foreign expansion, thereby strengthening the effectiveness of family business culture. At the same time, succession planning and openness to professionalization help mitigate the initial risks of internationalization and generate sustained performance over time (Costa et al.,

2022). However, Eddleston et al. (2019) caution that the adoption of innovative strategies, such as niche positioning, is insufficient if the company operates in institutionally weak contexts or lacks formal management practices.

Gamad (2019), analyzing Philippine family micro-enterprises, demonstrates that tools such as lean management and strategic quality management enhance organizational agility, thereby reducing operational risk in the early stages of internationalization. This approach enables companies to respond flexibly to dynamic and competitive environments. Similarly, Lobo et al. (2023) highlight that family SMEs with strong international networks, calibrated risk-taking capabilities, and a proactive market orientation achieve superior performance in foreign markets, thanks to reduced perceived risk and more ambitious entry strategies.

On a theoretical level, Madonna et al. (2025) note that, despite the growing focus on risk management in family businesses, there remains a lack of in-depth studies on the interaction between innovation and risk management. Family social capital and the capacity for innovation should be analyzed as synergistic levers for explaining international resilience. Finally, Ratten and Tajeddini (2017) emphasize the importance of responsiveness to international customer needs and a willingness to take risks as factors that accelerate internationalization. However, they also point to a widespread lack of proactivity in seeking new foreign opportunities, which may limit the growth potential of family businesses. In line with this, Ratten et al. (2017) argue that the integration of innovation and entrepreneurial orientation is essential for building a competitive and sustainable reputation in global markets.

## 6.4 Political Risk and Institutional Adaptation in Global Family Businesses

Political risk management and adaptation to the institutional context are complex challenges for family businesses engaged in internationalization, given their unique ownership and value structures. Jimenez et al. (2019) demonstrate that Spanish family-owned multinationals with strong family control—in terms of ownership and board representation—tend to avoid politically unstable markets; however, they still manage political risk effectively due to the social capital they have developed over time with local institutional actors. This relational approach also extends to the intra-family dimension, as family support, especially from entrepreneurial parents, increases self-efficacy in young entrepreneurs, strengthening their ability to cope with foreign political and cultural uncertainty (Gonzalez-Ramos et al., 2025).

Jorge et al. (2017) note that in small family businesses, direct management by the owners favors gradual expansion into institutionally and culturally similar markets, reducing exposure to external risks. In this context, Marín-Anglada et al. (2014) highlight that when ownership and control coincide, conservative strategies prevail; conversely, the entry of external managers favors more open approaches to political risk management. In this regard, Costa et al. (2022) observe that only family CEOs who are willing to delegate and to introduce external managerial skills can overcome inertia and embrace openness to global markets.

On the other hand, Miroshnychenko et al. (2023) highlight the heterogeneity of family businesses in their responses to sudden institutional reforms, showing that some defend their markets, whereas others accelerate internationalization to mitigate instability.

The role of external investors can accentuate or mitigate these dynamics. In the Indian context, Panicker et al. (2019) show that "pressure-sensitive" institutional investors curtail international strategies due to political risk concerns, whereas "pressure-resistant" investors support them, particularly when family ownership is strong, highlighting a strategic mediation between external pressures and family orientation. Finally, political risk management in family businesses is evolving from a reactive logic to a more resilient approach.

## 6.5 Discussion: Strengths and Vulnerabilities in International Risk Management

A key strength of family businesses in managing internationalization-related risk lies in their strategic prudence and long-term orientation. This attitude often translates into careful selection of entry modes into foreign markets, favoring less risky options such as franchising, greenfield investments, or equity alliances (Andreu et al., 2020; Chakraborty & Singla, 2025). This caution also extends to the currency sphere, where they prefer to limit exposure at source by reducing penetration in unstable markets or selecting less volatile currencies (Anderson et al., 2023).

A second strength is the ability of family businesses to build external relational capital, that is, relationships with institutional stakeholders, customers, suppliers, and local networks, which reduce political and institutional uncertainty (Jimenez et al., 2019; Gonzalez-Ramos et al., 2025). In unstable contexts, this relational capital represents a real competitive advantage in managing political risk and building local legitimacy. Family businesses should consider the intentional building of these relationships as an integral part of their international strategy, including through participation in business networks and public-private partnerships.

Structural resilience, fueled by a combination of family culture, entrepreneurial orientation, and adaptive innovation, should also be emphasized. Companies that invest in digitalization, lean management, and international networks are more agile and better able to cope with turbulent environments, thereby enhancing their capacity to manage external risks (Chatterjee et al., 2023; Gamad, 2019; Lobo et al., 2023).

Finally, generational diversity is an essential internal lever, as second generations, who are often better educated and more internationalized, are more inclined to take strategic risks and experiment with new modes of expansion (Fang et al., 2018; Petrù et al., 2019), providing a valuable counterbalance to the caution of the founders.

On the other hand, family structure can also be a constraint to effective risk management. A first obvious limitation is the reluctance to adopt formal risk management systems or to make structured use of currency hedging instruments, especially when the family has direct influence on management and internal trust and informality prevail (Hiebl et al., 2019). Companies should consider strengthening formal risk management mechanisms, particularly in contexts with high systemic risk exposure.

Furthermore, the concentration of family control can generate management problems: while it promotes caution, it can also lead to unsystematic, speculative behavior driven by overconfidence or excessive optimism among the founders (Aabo et al., 2011). This ambivalent behavior compromises the consistency of the risk management strategy. Family businesses should therefore strengthen their internal control systems, including the engagement of external advisors or audit committees tailored to internationalization.

A further limitation is cultural rigidity and a low propensity for proactivity, which inhibits the exploration of new foreign opportunities and can limit global competitiveness (Ratten & Tajeddini, 2017). This strategic passivity clashes with the urgency, in dynamic markets, to anticipate risks rather than react only defensively.

Succession management is also a challenge that is not always well addressed. In the absence of structured plans or openness to professionalization, companies risk becoming trapped in outdated management models that are ill-suited to managing risk in complex environments (Costa et al., 2022).

Finally, family businesses tend to avoid culturally and institutionally distant markets, thus limiting their potential for strategic expansion. The tendency to favor similar markets, while understandable from a prudential perspective, risks reducing growth opportunities and leaving high-profit strategic segments uncovered (Jorge et al., 2017; Miroshnychenko et al., 2023). It is therefore advisable to develop cultural learning strategies and more sophisticated country-risk assessment tools to enable a more strategic selection of international destinations.

From a theoretical perspective, the studies analyzed highlight the importance of an integrated approach that accounts for both socioemotional and institutional risk. The concept of mixed gamble (Lohe et al., 2021) suggests that family businesses do not simply react to risks, but incorporate them into their decision-making models, often in non-linear ways. This opens up the possibility of investigating how family resilience can be designed through succession, innovation, and dynamic governance (Lobo et al., 2023; Marín-Anglada et al., 2014).

## References

Aabo, T., Kuhn, J., & Zanotti, G. (2011). Founder family influence and foreign exchange risk management. *International Journal of Managerial Finance, 7*(1), 38–67.

Ali, S., Rehman, A. U., Jawad, M., & Naz, M. (2024). Product market competition and investment efficiency nexus with mediating effect of firm risk-taking in Pakistan. *International Journal of Disclosure and Governance, 21*(3), 488–499.

Anderson, R. C., Bergbrant, M. C., Hunter, D. M., & Reeb, D. M. (2023). Are founding families less willing to bear risk? Evidence from the currency exposure and internationalization strategy of family firms. *Financial Management, 52*(1), 41–66.

Andreu, R., Quer, D., & Rienda, L. (2020). The influence of family character on the choice of foreign market entry mode: An analysis of Spanish hotel chains. *European Research on Management and Business Economics, 26*(1), 40–44.

Boellis, A., Mariotti, S., Minichilli, A., & Piscitello, L. (2016). Family involvement and firms' establishment mode choice in foreign markets. *Journal of International Business Studies, 47*(8), 929–950.

Braga, V., Correia, A., Braga, A., & Lemos, S. (2017). The innovation and internationalisation processes of family businesses. *Review of International Business and Strategy, 27*(2), 231–247.

Chakraborty, S., & Singla, C. (2025). Navigating international entry via strategic alliances: Comparison of family and non-family firms. *Journal of International Management*, 101250.

Chatterjee, S., Chaudhuri, R., Vrontis, D., & Maalaoui, A. (2023). Internationalization of family business and its performance: Examining the moderating role of digitalization and international networking capability. *Review of Managerial Science, 17*(7), 2443–2470.

Chen, V. Z., Hobdari, B., Kellermanns, F. W., & Sluhan, A. (2022). For love or money? Family versus financial blockholders in international acquisitions. *Corporate Governance: An International Review, 30*(2), 140–160.

Claver, E., Rienda, L., & Quer, D. (2008). Family firms' risk perception: Empirical evidence on the internationalization process. *Journal of Small Business and Enterprise Development, 15*(3), 457–471.

Costa, A. D., Zen, A. C., & Spindler, E. D. S. (2022). Family succession, professionalization and internationalization: A study of Brazilian family businesses. *Journal of Family Business Management, 12*(4), 1065–1080.

D'Allura, G. M., Calabrò, A., Bannò, M., & Pisano, V. (2024). Family firms' equity entry modes: Bridging family business and international business. *Journal of Management & Organization*, 1–21.

de Groote, J., Feninger, M., & Kammerlander, N. (2023). Family firm internationalization and top management team collaboration: Roles, emotional attachment, and risk perceptions. *Journal of World Business, 58*(6), 101489.

Eddleston, K. A., Sarathy, R., & Banalieva, E. R. (2019). When a high-quality niche strategy is not enough to spur family-firm internationalization: The role of external and internal contexts. *Journal of International Business Studies, 50*(5), 783–808.

Fang, H., Kotlar, J., Memili, E., Chrisman, J. J., & De Massis, A. (2018). The pursuit of international opportunities in family firms: Generational differences and the role of knowledge-based resources. *Global Strategy Journal, 8*(1), 136–157.

Gamad, L. C. (2019). Governing company performance agility through strategic quality management principles and lean business practices: Evidences and challenges for the business industry in the Philippines. *Review of Integrative Business and Economics Research, 8*(4), 17.

González-Ramos, M. I., Guadamillas, F., Ortiz, B., & Donate, M. J. (2025). Antecedents of entrepreneurial intention in an international business environment: A gender comparison. *International Journal of Entrepreneurial Behavior & Research, 31*(6), 1543–1575.

Hasenau, A. F., & Dutzi, A. (2023). Impact of risk culture on supplier selection decisions in family firms. *Journal of Strategy and Management, 16*(4), 630–642.

Hiebl, M. R., Duller, C., & Neubauer, H. (2019). Enterprise risk management in family firms: Evidence from Austria and Germany. *The Journal of Risk Finance, 20*(1), 39–58.

Jimenez, A., Majocchi, A., & Piana, B. D. (2019). Not all family firms are equal: The moderating effect of family involvement on the political risk exposure of the foreign direct investment portfolio. Preliminary evidence from Spanish multinational enterprises. *Thunderbird International Business Review, 61*(2), 309–323.

Jorge, M., Couto, M., Veloso, T., & Franco, M. (2017). When family businesses go international: management sets the path. *Journal of Business Strategy, 38*(1), 31–38.

Lobo, C. A., Fernandes, C., Ferreira, J., Veiga, P. M., & Gerschewski, S. (2023). The determinants of international performance for family firms: Understanding the effects of resources, capabilities, and market orientation. *Entrepreneurship Research Journal, 13*(3), 773–811.

Lohe, F. W., Calabrò, A., & Torchia, M. (2021). Disentangling the drivers of family firms internationalization through the lens of socioemotional wealth. *Journal of International Entrepreneurship, 19*(4), 479–509.

Madonna, S., Cestari, G., & Georgiev, M. G. (2025). Unveiling risk management dynamics in family businesses through a bibliometric analysis. *Journal of Family Business Management.* https://doi.org/10.1108/JFBM-09-2024-0231

Marín Anglada, Q., Campa-Planas, F., & Hernández Lara, A. B. (2014). Uncertainty in the family business facing the process of internationalization: Literature review and future research agenda. *Intangible Capital, 10*(4), 836–853.

Mazzelli, A., Miller, D., Le Breton-Miller, I., De Massis, A., & Kotlar, J. (2023). Outcome-based imitation in family firms' international market entry decisions. *Entrepreneurship Theory and Practice, 47*(4), 1059–1092.

Miroshnychenko, I., Eddleston, K. A., & De Massis, A. (2023). Fight or flight? Understanding family firm internationalization when the rules of the game change. *Journal of World Business, 58*(5), 101462.

Monreal-Pérez, J., & Sánchez-Marín, G. (2017). Does transitioning from family to non-family controlled firm influence internationalization? *Journal of Small Business and Enterprise Development, 24*(4), 775–792.

Panicker, V. S., Mitra, S., & Upadhyayula, R. S. (2019). Institutional investors and international investments in emerging economy firms: A behavioral risk perspective. *Journal of World Business, 54*(4), 322–334.

Petrů, N., Tomášková, A., & Krošláková, M. (2019). Diversification of export territories of family businesses as a tool of their further development. *Problems and Perspectives in Management, 17*(3), 306.

Ratten, V., & Tajeddini, K. (2017). Innovativeness in family firms: An internationalization approach. *Review of International Business and Strategy, 27*(2), 217–230.

Ratten, V., Ramadani, V., Dana, L. P., Hoy, F., & Ferreira, J. (2017). Family entrepreneurship and internationalization strategies. *Review of International Business and Strategy, 27*(2), 150–160.

Rienda, L., Claver, E., Quer, D., & Andreu, R. (2019). Family businesses from emerging markets and choice of entry mode abroad: Insights from Indian firms. *Asian Business & Management, 18*(1), 6–30.

Şahin, K., Artan, S., & Tuysuz, S. (2015). The moderating effects of a board of directors on FDI's international diversification in Turkey. *International Journal of Organizational Analysis, 23*(1), 61–88.

Saurabh, K., & Kumar, V. (2025). Descendant CEOs and cross-border acquisitions in family firms: The moderating role of family involvement. *Long Range Planning*, 102538.

# Chapter 7
# SEW, Reputation, ESG, and Risk

**Abstract** This chapter examines the role of affective dimensions and reputation in family business risk management, drawing on two complementary perspectives. On the one hand, it explores the link between emotional dimension and decision-making behavior (Emotional dimension and risk-purple cluster), highlighting how identity values, affective relationships, and non-economic goals influence risk perception and adaptability in the face of uncertainty. The analysis highlights the ambivalence of these intangible assets, which can both strengthen family resilience and hinder innovation and strategic planning. On the other hand, the chapter examines the interactions among risk management, reputation, and corporate social responsibility (Risk Management, Reputation, and CSR in Family Businesses-green cluster), emphasizing that ESG practices are often adopted reactively, influenced by institutional context, governance composition, and stakeholder pressure. Reputation emerges as a crucial lever for reducing uncertainty and strengthening legitimacy, but also as a potential source of vulnerability when inconsistencies exist between stated values and practices.

**Keywords** Socioemotional wealth · Reputation · CSR · Stakeholder pressure · Identity · Risk management

## 7.1 Reputation and Risk Management

Reputation emerges as a key strategic asset in family business risk management, serving as both a defensive lever and relational capital that must be actively protected. Several studies demonstrate that reputation serves as a mechanism for mitigating uncertainty among key stakeholders, particularly in markets with high information risk. For example, Allison and Anglin (2025) demonstrate that, in crowdfunding campaigns, the company's family identity serves as a positive reputational signal, enhancing investor confidence and improving fundraising performance. However, reputation is also fragile and vulnerable to inconsistent or perceived hypocritical behavior; Choi et al. (2024) highlight how inconsistent social



A. M. Moisello, P. Gottardo, *Risk and Sustainability in Family Businesses*, SpringerBriefs in Finance, https://doi.org/10.1007/978-3-032-19995-9_7

responsibility practices in Korean family businesses undermine legitimacy, thereby increasing reputational and strategic risk.

The link between reputation and risk management is also evident in CSR, which is often used as a risk-mitigation tool. However, Ma (2023) demonstrates how Chinese family businesses utilize CSR reporting not only to signal their ethical commitment but also to shield themselves from institutional threats, such as state intervention, by adopting international standards to enhance their legitimacy. Similarly, Özbay et al. (2023) find that Turkish family businesses opportunistically use CSR to offset the adverse reputational effects of aggressive tax avoidance. In these cases, CSR becomes an integral part of a reputational risk management strategy rather than a genuine expression of ethical values.

Family succession can also expose companies to significant reputational risks, as intergenerational altruism can lead to opportunistic behavior such as earnings management, with negative consequences for the company's transparency and reputation (Fang et al., 2021). Doluca et al. (2018) highlight a more cautious time strategy and a progressive approach to reputational risk, whereby an initially limited environmental commitment grows over time, reducing behavioral volatility and enhancing reputation in the long term.

In financial markets, reputation directly affects the cost of capital and visibility. Wu et al. (2014) demonstrate that Taiwanese family businesses with a high level of CSR commitment incur significantly lower capital costs, mainly due to investors' perception of lower risk. Yang et al. (2023) confirm that CSR also reduces stock price crash risk, more effectively in family businesses, due to their interest in preserving financial stability and maintaining transparent communication. However, Luo et al. (2019) show that family businesses in emerging markets may suffer from an ex ante reputational deficiency, as international financial analysts cover them less frequently, particularly when they are from countries with shareholder-oriented institutions, reflecting a perceived bias against family governance risk.

Finally, Vijayagopal and Thenmozhi (2025) show that in family businesses in emerging markets, share pledging behavior represents a trade-off between protecting reputation and control and the need to raise capital for growth. However, overly casual pledge management can weaken investor confidence, increasing internal systemic risk.

## 7.2 ESG and Risk Management

Several studies suggest that the ESG commitment of family businesses is often driven by risk management considerations rather than genuine social motivation. Abeysekera and Fernando (2020) show that these companies invest in environmentally responsible practices only when they perceive direct benefits for shareholders, and avoid purely social initiatives unless they are functional for reducing business or reputational risk. This behavior is explained by Type I and Type II agency theory, which highlights how internal dynamics among managers, shareholders, and controlling families shape strategic selectivity in the adoption of environmentally responsible practices.

Inclusion, particularly gender inclusion, is a potential lever for more sustainability-oriented governance; however, the results are mixed. Khidmat et al. (2022) and Jouber (2024) demonstrate that female board membership is associated with greater adoption of socially responsible practices and reduced business risks, including default risk. However, this effect is limited by company size, state ownership, or tokenism, as reported by Oussii and Jeriji (2025), who argue that in family businesses, diversity is sometimes adopted symbolically, with no concrete effects on performance or environmental sustainability. Despite this, Domańska et al. (2024) highlight that female CEOs can serve as transformative agents of more authentic CSR, thereby strengthening the link between entrepreneurial orientation and sustainability.

From a financial perspective, social and environmental commitments can serve as an essential mechanism for reducing perceived risk for investors and creditors. Duggal et al. (2024) show that mandatory CSR compliance in India reduces the cost of debt, albeit with mitigated effects in family businesses led by non-founding CEOs. Similarly, Wu et al. (2014) and Yang et al. (2023) highlight that CSR combined with accounting transparency and concentrated family leadership reduces the cost of capital and the risk of stock crashes. However, in the presence of opportunistic practices such as earnings management, the instrumental use of CSR can increase reputational risk, as noted by Jian et al. (2024).

The presence of external governance mechanisms can positively influence the effectiveness of CSR as a risk management tool. Bansal et al. (2018) find that CSR disclosure is higher when the board includes independent members, but only when family ownership coexists, which reassures the authenticity of the information and integrates agency theory and socioemotional wealth theory. Similarly, Benkraiem et al. (2022) demonstrate that institutional investors with cross-shareholdings serve as CSR controllers, thereby limiting opportunistic behavior. However, business risk can inhibit CSR commitment, as Syed and Butt (2017) demonstrate that in the presence of high economic risks, family businesses tend to reduce social inclusion initiatives, favoring asset preservation.

Finally, the strategic orientation of family businesses affects the adoption of CSR. Häußler and Ulrich (2024) identify three strategic clusters: family values, stakeholders, and innovation, which integrate sustainability and risk management. In contrast, Saeed et al. (2016) emphasize that gender diversity is favored in large family businesses with lower risk exposure. However, the effect of generations is controversial. According to Yang et al. (2023), first-generation family leadership enhances CSR effectiveness, whereas the second generation appears less aware of the reputational value of sustainability.

## 7.3 Risk and Institutional Contexts

Risk management dynamics assume a particularly complex connotation in family businesses operating in emerging markets, where institutional weaknesses, information opacity, and regulatory instability heighten the strategic value of reputation and render ESG a tool of legitimization that is often more reactive than transformative. Risk management in family businesses operating in emerging markets is a multidimensional challenge, strongly influenced by the institutional context, ownership structure, and relational capital. In environments characterized by regulatory instability, information opacity, and weak investor protection, entrepreneurial families adopt risk management strategies that prioritize prudence, asset protection, and reputation preservation. As illustrated by Chakrabarti and Mondal (2020), institutional reforms in India alter perceived risk and reduce families' entrepreneurial orientation, thereby diminishing risk appetite. This behavior is interpreted through institutional theory, which links the regulatory context to the strategic decisions of family businesses.

A specific dimension of risk management in these contexts concerns succession risk management. Al-Zaqeba et al. (2024) demonstrate that, in Middle Eastern countries, the sustainability of family businesses hinges on their capacity to integrate strategic planning and innovation to address the risks associated with intergenerational transmission within an unstable regulatory environment. Dependence on family networks, a characteristic of Asian relational systems, can also lead to vulnerability. As Fan et al. (2025) demonstrate, although these networks provide proper protection against external shocks, they discourage long-term financial planning, thereby exposing the company to unmanaged future risks.

Gega et al. (2024, 2025) highlight that European agri-food family businesses, despite exhibiting a long-term orientation, do not consistently achieve ESG advantages over non-family companies due to their lower risk appetite. Liu and Zhang (2024) confirm that, in China, family businesses with strong ESG scores exhibit a lower default risk; however, this effect is mitigated by family concentration on the board of directors, which reduces the effectiveness of sustainable practices due to nepotistic dynamics.

In contexts where investor protection is weak, as in many emerging markets, ESG can be used instrumentally to reduce regulatory pressure. Martínez-Ferrero et al. (2016) highlight that, in these cases, corporate social responsibility acts as an entrenchment mechanism, protecting dominant families from external pressures but generating high reputational risk. This risk manifests as financial instability, as shown by Rasheed et al. (2025) in Pakistan, where family businesses are unable to prevent stock price crashes due to the absence of institutional investor controls.

The environmental and regulatory response is also influenced by risk perception. Szymczyk and Włodarczyk (2025) reveal that, in Poland, only family businesses operating in environmentally sensitive sectors rigorously adopt green practices in response to regulatory pressure and geopolitical shocks, confirming that contextual sensitivity drives the adoption of risk-mitigation strategies. Finally, Wu et al. (2014)

and Yang et al. (2023) demonstrate that in emerging markets, ESG reduces the cost of capital and the risk of stock market crashes more significantly than in developed markets, as it enhances transparency and mitigates information asymmetry.

## 7.4 Socioemotional Wealth and Risk

Non-financial objectives, particularly the preservation of socioemotional wealth, as well as psychological and relational factors, play a decisive role in risk management and strategy definition in family businesses, especially during generational transitions and in highly uncertain contexts (Bang et al., 2023). SEW represents emotional and symbolic capital, comprising identity, family ties, reputation, and control, the protection of which can significantly influence management choices that are profoundly shaped by risk aversion (Gomez-Mejia et al., 2011). Gomez-Mejia et al. (2007) demonstrate that Spanish family businesses, when considering international diversification, tend to reject economically advantageous options that involve a loss of control, precisely to protect the SEW. This highlights behavior that is apparently "irrational" in economic terms but perfectly consistent with an affective-identity logic. The value of this study lies in making explicit the existence of perceived affective capital that functions as a 'cognitive constraint' and a decision-making filter, altering perceptions of risk and shifting the threshold for acceptable trade-offs between economic risk and symbolic loss. As subsequent studies (Gomez-Mejia et al., 2024) have shown, in organizational and strategic environments characterized by instability and complexity, Latin American family businesses tend to become SEW-intensive and SEW-sensitive, reacting strongly to any perceived threat to their affective wealth and adopting defensive or, at times, highly reactive strategies. According to Shen (2018), when the family perceives an imminent risk of SEW erosion, it may paradoxically adopt aggressive strategies, such as diversification, to safeguard its long-term family identity.

The ambivalent nature of SEW is also evident in the relationship between entrepreneurial orientation and performance. Hernández-Linares et al. (2020) show that, in the presence of a strong motivation to preserve SEW, risk-taking may be encouraged, while innovation perceived as a threat to symbolic and cultural stability may be inhibited. Similarly, Oke et al. (2025) emphasize that founders and successors view sustainable innovation as a lever for strengthening their family's reputation, but diverge in how they balance costs, benefits, and reputational risks. In this perspective, Penney et al. (2019) propose that SEW operates as a cognitive and unconscious filter, directing strategy toward alternatives that appear more consistent with family values.

This orientation is also influenced by deep psychological dynamics, which are particularly evident during succession processes. In this sense, Gundolf et al. (2013) highlight how fear of losing power, being forgotten, or identity can lead founders to postpone leadership transitions, fueling latent tensions and hindering effective planning. Intergenerational trust is a key element, but it can be easily undermined when successors deviate from the family's historical values, creating emotional and organizational rifts that increase strategic uncertainty (Jayantilal et al., 2015). Furthermore, the fear of opportunistic behavior by external managers often leads to the selection of family successors, even if they are less competent, to avoid the risk of losing accumulated human and relational capital (Lee et al., 2003).

The transition requires relational skills such as delegation, open-mindedness, and clear communication to build trust and ensure continuity (Samei & Feyzbakhsh, 2015). The lack of explicit communication observed by Staehr (2015) can prolong uncertainty and reduce organizational cohesion. From an evolutionary perspective, Sundaramurthy (2008) cautions that trust, although initially conferring a competitive advantage, tends to erode as the company expands if formal structures, transparent processes, and inclusive governance do not underpin it.

Furthermore, the internal family configuration affects risk propensity: close family ties are associated with greater risk aversion. At the same time, more distant relationships, such as those between cousins or uncles, tend to favor greater flexibility (Tan et al., 2024). Wang et al. (2024) also demonstrate that father-son co-management limits investment in green innovation, not only due to financial constraints but also due to perceptions that such innovations are too risky or foreign to established family values.

Finally, as suggested by Salas-Paramo and Escandon-Barbosa (2025), the adoption of proactive and strategic management of SEW, involving stakeholders and providing formal planning tools, can transform non-financial objectives from a brake to a lever for organizational resilience.

## 7.5 Generational Transitions and Strategic Risk

Succession is one of the most critical and risky phases in the life of family businesses, profoundly affecting business continuity and the ability to cope with uncertainty. The intergenerational transition process is not just a formal transfer of power, but a complex reconfiguration of leadership, identity, and risk strategies (Li et al., 2023). According to Carter III and Justis (2009), the success of succession depends on the transformation of the successor from "follower" to authentic leader, an evolution facilitated by the quality of the parent-child relationship, the gradual assumption of responsibility, and long-term orientation. However, as Chalus-Sauvannet et al. (2016) note, in some cases, children take over only after gaining external professional experience, leading to more legitimate and innovation-oriented leadership.

Strategic succession planning and the quality of institutional regulation are crucial in mitigating succession risks (Al-Zaqeba et al., 2024). Internal family dynamics are a critical factor, as a lack of cultural alignment and sibling rivalry can undermine post-succession stability (Jayantilal et al., 2015, 2016). Succession generates tensions between family dynamics, characterized by emotional ties and the pursuit of stability, and business needs in terms of innovation and efficiency, necessitating a delicate balance to ensure continuity and resilience (Meier & Thelisson, 2020). However, many companies fail to address succession challenges promptly by not preparing a structured succession plan, thereby exposing themselves to a significant risk of organizational failure (Rumanko et al., 2021).

In succession processes, Zhang and Wei (2025) find that successors tend to slow down digital transformations, fearing that they may alter the family identity. Putri and Viverita (2019) demonstrate that hereditary CEOs tend to avoid risky strategies, preferring conservative approaches that aim to protect socioemotional wealth (SEW), even at the expense of limiting growth. Therefore, in highly volatile sectors, family businesses often opt for external managers to enhance performance and mitigate the risks associated with family continuity (Yeh & Liao, 2021). This is echoed by Yeh (2019), who links good corporate governance to a lower probability of inefficient family succession, emphasizing the importance of the institutional environment in containing risk.

Finally, Thevenard-Puthod (2022) proposes the 'hybrid succession teams' model, which combines family and non-family members in the transition to reduce information asymmetry and improve risk management, highlighting that if the predecessor's preferences for relatives prevail, the likelihood of conflict and failure increases. In extreme cases, such as the Reliance case analyzed by Saxena (2013), inheritance controversies not only undermine the company but can also generate systemic risks that impact the entire economic system.

## 7.6 Family Leadership and Entrepreneurial Risk: Identity, Generation, and CEO Styles

Family involvement and the presence of family CEOs play a central role in the strategic and risk management dynamics of family businesses, influencing both entrepreneurial choices and long-term stability. Casillas and Moreno (2010) show how high family involvement positively moderates the relationship between entrepreneurial orientation and growth, making innovation and risk-taking more effective only in the presence of a cohesive and actively involved family. However, the same involvement can act as a brake on entrepreneurship when the desire to preserve control and socioemotional wealth prevails, as evidenced by the fact that family CEOs, in situations of negative performance, tend to favor conservative retrenchment strategies (Casillas et al., 2019).

The link between family leadership and strategic transformation appears ambivalent. On the one hand, He et al. (2025) demonstrate that founder leadership can foster bold strategies, such as digitalization, particularly in less conservative cultural contexts and in the absence of state interference. On the other hand, Zheng et al. (2023) highlight that, in anticipation of future family succession, founders adopt more cautious behaviors such as reducing R&D investments and increasing liquidity to mitigate volatility and facilitate a smooth intergenerational transition.

The risk orientation of family CEOs also varies by generation, with descendants tending to be more risk-averse than founders, preferring small-scale international acquisitions, mainly if the board is dominated by family members (Kraiczy et al., 2015). In such cases, the presence of independent board members can mitigate caution and favor more expansive strategies.

The risk issue is further influenced by gender identity. Zona et al. (2024) show that female family CEOs adopt different risk-taking behaviors than their male counterparts: they are more daring when performance falls below expectations, perhaps to counter stereotypes and legitimize themselves, but more conservative when performance exceeds expectations. Finally, according to Revilla et al. (2016), strong family involvement in management can reduce the risk of failure, particularly during economic crises. However, excessive entrepreneurship can undermine this protective effect by eroding family cohesion and increasing risk exposure. In summary, family involvement and the leadership of family CEOs are a powerful but ambivalent strategic lever, whose effectiveness depends on contingent factors such as the stage of the life cycle, the composition of the board, the generation in charge, and the willingness to professionalize governance.

## 7.7 Reputational and Emotional Capital in Risk Management: Evidence and Implications for Family Businesses

This section offers a critical discussion of the main findings from the literature on the interaction between risk management, reputational capital, and the affective dimension in family businesses. The discussion is divided into two subsections: the first investigates the relationship among risk, reputation, and ESG, highlighting the mechanisms by which family businesses build and defend their legitimacy, in light of institutional pressures and stakeholder expectations. The second focuses on the affective and symbolic assets that characterize family businesses, analyzing their ambivalent role in building resilience, managing succession, and risk tolerance. In both cases, theoretical and managerial implications are developed to clarify the conditions under which these resources are effective in strengthening the sustainability and adaptive capacity of family businesses.

### *7.7.1 The Relationship Between Risk and ESG*

One of the main strengths lies in the centrality of reputation as intangible capital and a lever of trust toward the market, stakeholders, and investors (Allison & Anglin, 2025). The propensity of family businesses to protect their identity through consistent reputational strategies, such as the targeted use of ESG, is associated with a perceived reduction in risk and improved financial conditions (Wu et al., 2014; Yang et al., 2023). This advantage is amplified in opaque or unstable markets, such as emerging markets, where ESG can serve as a signal of reliability and transparency (Wu et al., 2014).

A second strength concerns intergenerational adaptability and long-term vision. In contexts of succession or institutional change, families sometimes employ a progressive and prudent risk-management strategy, as highlighted by Doluca et al. (2018) and Al-Zaqeba et al. (2024). Entrepreneurial families can also mobilize relational networks and social capital to mitigate uncertainties related to the institutional context or economic cycles (Fan et al., 2025; Liu & Zhang, 2024).

Finally, strategic flexibility in governance, when accompanied by selective openness, for example, to the entry of independent members or female leadership, can strengthen the effectiveness of ESG as a risk management tool, as demonstrated by the findings of Bansal et al. (2018) and Jouber (2024).

Despite these strengths, significant vulnerabilities emerge, foremost among them the instrumentalization of ESG and reputation. In many cases, family businesses adopt social and environmental practices not out of ethical conviction, but to compensate for questionable behavior (tax avoidance, earnings management, share pledges), thereby increasing reputational risk if these inconsistencies come to light (Özbay et al., 2023; Fang et al., 2021; Jian et al., 2024).

A further weakness is the selective inclusion: many family businesses adopt gender diversity or board independence practices symbolically, with no substantive impact on governance or risk management (Chaabouni et al., 2025; Oussii & Jeriji, 2025). In these cases, inclusion becomes a formal exercise that undermines the authenticity of the company's ethical stance.

In emerging markets, the primary limitation is excessive ownership concentration and the absence of external controls, which can lead to opacity, agency conflicts, and inefficiencies in risk management, as demonstrated by Rasheed et al. (2025) and Martínez-Ferrero et al. (2016) in other settings.

Overall, family businesses have reputational, relational, and strategic resources that, if managed consistently and transparently, are powerful assets for addressing reputational, financial, and systemic risks. However, these resources can become sources of vulnerability when coupled with opportunistic behavior, governance deficits, or excessive organizational closure. The crucial challenge for the future is to transform these defensive levers into proactive tools for sustainability, inclusion, and resilience, avoiding instrumental drifts and strengthening internal and external accountability mechanisms.

The relationship among reputation, ESG, and risk management in family businesses is complex, encompassing organizational, institutional, and intergenerational dynamics. First, reputation emerges as an intangible strategic asset that serves as both a mechanism for reducing uncertainty among external stakeholders and a lever for securing more favorable financial conditions, particularly in markets with high information risk (Allison & Anglin, 2025; Wu et al., 2014). This implies an extension of socioemotional wealth theory, insofar as protecting reputation becomes not only an affective goal but also instrumental to the stability and sustainability of the company (Yang et al., 2023). However, such reputational capital can become a strategic vulnerability if ESG is adopted instrumentally, through practices inconsistent with stated values, resulting in ethical misalignments and increased reputational risk (Choi et al., 2024; Özbay et al., 2023; Jian et al., 2024).

From a theoretical perspective, evidence suggests that ESG in family businesses does not respond solely to altruistic motives, but is often influenced by agency dynamics and institutional pressures, particularly in emerging contexts (Abeysekera & Fernando, 2020; Martínez-Ferrero et al., 2016). In such environments, ESG assumes an ambivalent role: on the one hand, it serves as a tool for legitimization and the mitigation of regulatory risk; on the other hand, it can consolidate dominant positions and protect family power structures, according to entrenchment logic (Rasheed et al., 2025). Institutional theories, therefore, help understand how the regulatory and cultural contexts shape the strategic choices of family businesses regarding risk, reputation, and sustainability (Chakrabarti & Mondal, 2020; Szymczyk & Włodarczyk, 2025).

From a managerial perspective, family businesses are called upon to transform reputation management from a defensive function to a proactive lever for sustainability and resilience. This involves integrating ESG into corporate culture and decision-making processes, avoiding opportunistic or symbolic approaches, such as adopting non-substantial gender diversity or ethical communication that is disconnected from actual behavior (Oussii & Jeriji, 2025; Chaabouni et al., 2025). The effective inclusion of independent members on boards and openness to non-traditional leadership, such as female CEOs or external managers, can strengthen the credibility of ESG initiatives and enhance risk management by addressing cognitive biases and self-referential dynamics typically associated with family governance (Jouber, 2024; Bansal et al., 2018).

For stakeholders, consistency between stated values and actual practices is a key criterion for trust. Evidence shows that ESG perceived as authentic reduces the cost of capital and mitigates the risk of share price collapse, benefiting investors and creditors (Wu et al., 2014; Yang et al., 2023; Duggal et al., 2024). However, in emerging markets, biases about family governance and limited analyst coverage can penalize family businesses ex ante, creating a reputational gap that requires proactive communication and transparency (Luo et al., 2019).

For regulators and policymakers, evidence suggests the need for policies that incentivize authentic ESG behavior and penalize greenwashing or symbolic inclusion practices. Targeted regulatory interventions, such as mandatory disclosure of environmental, social, and governance practices, could enhance information quality and reduce asymmetry between family businesses and investors, particularly in contexts with weak institutional frameworks (Saeed et al., 2016; Liu & Zhang, 2024). At the same time, policymakers should recognize the positive role of family social capital in strengthening the resilience and legitimacy of the firm by promoting instruments that enhance the long-term orientation and territorial identity of family businesses.

### 7.7.2 *Affective Endowment and Risk*

The focus on non-financial objectives, the centrality of affective ties, and the configuration of leadership are both strengths and weaknesses in risk management. On the one hand, elements such as socioemotional wealth, intergenerational trust, and direct family involvement are valuable resources for building resilience, limiting exposure to financial risks, and strengthening organizational cohesion in critical moments, such as market crises or generational transitions. For example, attachment to family reputation and the desire for continuity help consolidate prudent defensive strategies, foster a long-term vision, and contain opportunistic behavior by external actors (Gomez-Mejia et al., 2024; Hernández-Linares et al., 2020; Salas-Paramo & Escandon-Barbosa, 2025). Furthermore, as observed in cases of father-son co-management or the presence of female CEOs, family identity can foster responsible and cautious behavior, thereby reducing systemic risk and enhancing business stability (Wang et al., 2024; Zona et al., 2024).

However, these same elements can constitute vulnerabilities, notably when adequate governance tools are lacking. The priority given to SEW can lead to excessive risk aversion, retrenchment strategies in times of difficulty, or the exclusion of more competent external figures, resulting in lost opportunities for growth or innovation (Casillas et al., 2019; Putri & Viverita, 2019; Zhang & Wei, 2025). Psychological factors, such as fear of oblivion or reluctance to relinquish power, can hinder effective succession planning and delay decision-making, thereby amplifying uncertainty and compromising continuity (Gundolf et al., 2013; Staehr, 2015). Furthermore, the lack of formalization of decision-making processes, typical of highly family-owned businesses, can exacerbate information asymmetries, particularly in contexts where leadership is characterized by close family ties (Samei & Feyzbakhsh, 2015; Sundaramurthy, 2008). The result is an organization that is potentially less adaptable to external changes, where emotional logic prevails over economic logic.

Ultimately, the board's generational composition and structure significantly affect risk tolerance. While founders often exhibit greater entrepreneurial boldness (He et al., 2025), successors tend toward more conservative strategies, slowing innovation and digital transformation, particularly when called upon to protect the family identity during the transition (Zheng et al., 2023; Tan et al., 2024). However, when these same successors have external professional experience or are supported by hybrid teams, greater risk management capacity and improved post-succession performance are observed (Chalus-Sauvannet et al., 2016; Thevenard-Puthod, 2022). Therefore, the strength of family businesses lies in cohesion, trust, and long-term vision, but their fragility emerges when these same traits prevent strategic adaptation, openness to professionalization, and proactive risk management consistent with the evolving competitive environment.

The emergence of socioemotional wealth as a dual-edged lever in risk management within family businesses necessitates revising traditional theoretical models. Evidence suggests that SEW does not operate as a single construct. Still, it is articulated across multiple cognitive and symbolic dimensions, including identity, control, reputation, and family ties (Berrone et al., 2012), which selectively influence risk-taking, entrepreneurial orientation, and succession choices. In theory, it is crucial to develop frameworks that disaggregate and analyze these dimensions, thereby overcoming monolithic approaches and valuing differences across generations, genders, and family configurations. Furthermore, the interaction between SEW and the institutional context suggests the need to integrate cultural and regulatory elements into risk and performance models, bridging the gap between affective and rational logic.

At the managerial level, the literature suggests strategically channeling SEW to enhance risk management, particularly in succession. Family businesses should adopt formal succession-planning tools and integrate governance mechanisms that balance affectivity and rational decision-making. In this regard, solutions such as "hybrid succession teams" (Thevenard-Puthod, 2022) and family-financial advisory models (Staehr, 2015) have proven effective in reducing conflict, improving transparency, and ensuring continuity. Experience and generational composition, as well as the presence of female CEOs, influence risk appetite in ways that are both distinct and often counterintuitive, suggesting that entrepreneurship metrics should be redefined to account for cultural sensitivity, gender, and leadership styles.

Technological adoption and digital transformation, often perceived as threats to SEW, require a strategic narrative that reconnects them to the company's founding values. In this sense, it is crucial to promote a vision of sustainability and innovation as a continuity of values rather than a break with identity. Finally, the heterogeneity of family ties suggests that strategic flexibility increases with less dense configurations of emotional ties. The presence of independent advisors and pluralistic governance thus emerges as a key tool for managing information asymmetries, mitigating risk, and enhancing resilience.

## References

Abeysekera, A. P., & Fernando, C. S. (2020). Corporate social responsibility versus corporate shareholder responsibility: A family firm perspective. *Journal of Corporate Finance, 61*, 101370.

Allison, T. H., & Anglin, A. H. (2025). The power of family firm image in rewards-based crowdfunding. *Journal of Small Business Management*, 1–34.

Al-Zaqeba, M. A. A., Alshehadeh, A. R., Al-Khawaja, H. A., Basheti, I. A., & Lootah, R. E. S. A. (2024). The role of inheritance risk management in family enterprises to achieve family businesses sustainability in the middle east. *Humanities and Social Sciences Letters, 12*(3), 639–658.

Bang, N. P., Calabrò, A., & Valentino, A. (2023). Strategic transitions: Unraveling the impact of socioemotional wealth and generational cohorts on succession planning in family SMEs. *International Journal of Entrepreneurial Behavior & Research, 30*(1), 23–51.

Bansal, S., Lopez-Perez, M. V., & Rodriguez-Ariza, L. (2018). Board independence and corporate social responsibility disclosure: The mediating role of the presence of family ownership. *Administrative Sciences, 8*(3), 33.

Benkraiem, R., Hamza, T., Lakhal, F., & Nizar, H. (2022). Family control, institutional cross holding and corporate social responsibility. *Economics Bulletin, 42*(4), 2231–2247.

Berrone, P., Cruz, C., & Gomez-Mejia, L. R. (2012). Socioemotional wealth in family firms: Theoretical dimensions, assessment approaches, and agenda for future research. *Family Business Review, 25*(3), 258–279.

Carter, J., III, & Justis, R. (2009). The development of successors from followers to leaders in small family firms. *Family Business Review, 22*(2), 109–124.

Casillas, J. C., & Moreno, A. M. (2010). The relationship between entrepreneurial orientation and growth: The moderating role of family involvement. *Entrepreneurship & Regional Development, 22*(3–4), 265–291.

Casillas, J. C., Moreno-Menéndez, A. M., Barbero, J. L., & Clinton, E. (2019). Retrenchment strategies and family involvement: The role of survival risk. *Family Business Review, 32*(1), 58–75.

Chaabouni, I., Ben Mbarek, N., & Ayadi, E. (2025). Do ESG Risk scores and board attributes impact corporate performance? Evidence from Saudi-listed companies. *Journal of Risk and Financial Management, 18*(2), 83.

Chakrabarti, A. B., & Mondal, A. (2020). The effect of institutional transition on entrepreneurial orientation of family businesses: Evidence from India. *International Journal of Entrepreneurial Behavior & Research, 26*(1), 76–97.

Chalus-Sauvannet, M. C., Deschamps, B., & Cisneros, L. (2016). Unexpected succession: When children return to take over the family business. *Journal of Small Business Management, 54*(2), 714–731.

Choi, J., Roh, T., & Lee, J. H. (2024). The pitfalls of corporate social irresponsibility: Hypocrisy of family firms in South Korea. *Journal of Cleaner Production, 435*, 140557.

Doluca, H., Wagner, M., & Block, J. (2018). Sustainability and environmental behaviour in family firms: A longitudinal analysis of environment-related activities, innovation and performance. *Business Strategy and the Environment, 27*(1), 152–172.

Domańska, A., Hernández-Linares, R., Zajkowski, R., & Żukowska, B. (2024). Family firm entrepreneurship and sustainability initiatives: Women as corporate change agents. *Business Ethics, the Environment & Responsibility, 33*(2), 217–240.

Duggal, N., He, L., & Shaw, T. S. (2024). Mandatory corporate social responsibility spending, family control, and the cost of debt. *The British Accounting Review, 101356.*

Fan, Y., Wang, Y., & Yang, Z. (2025). Risk-sharing networks, consumption, and asset allocation: Micro-evidence from China. *Emerging Markets Review, 66*, 101289.

Fang, H. C., Shi, Y., & Wu, Z. (2021). Familial altruism and reputation risk: Evidence from China. *China Finance Review International, 11*(4), 437–448.

Gega, M., Höhler, J., Bijman, J., & Oude Lansink, A. (2025). Firm ownership and ESG performance in European agri-food companies: The mediating effect of risk-taking and time horizon. *Corporate Social Responsibility and Environmental Management, 32*(1), 1161–1181.

Gega, M., Höhler, J., Bijman, J., & Oude Lansink, A. G. (2024). The relationship of firm ownership structure and sustainability performance in agri-food chains: A systematic literature review. *Cleaner Logistics and Supply Chain, 13*, 100193.

Gomez-Mejia, L. R., Cruz, C., Berrone, P., & De Castro, J. (2011). The bind that ties: Socioemotional wealth preservation in family firms. *Academy of Management Annals, 5*(1), 653–707.

Gómez-Mejía, L. R., Haynes, K. T., Núñez-Nickel, M., Jacobson, K. J., & Moyano-Fuentes, J. (2007). Socioemotional wealth and business risks in family-controlled firms: Evidence from Spanish olive oil mills. *Administrative Science Quarterly, 52*(1), 106–137.

Gomez-Mejia, L. R., Mendoza-Lopez, A., Cruz, C., Duran, P., & Aguinis, H. (2024). Socioemotional wealth in volatile, uncertain, complex, and ambiguous contexts: The case of family firms in Latin America and the Caribbean. *Journal of Family Business Strategy, 15*(1), 100551.

Gundolf, K., Meier, O., & Missonier, A. (2013). Transmission of family businesses in France. *International Journal of Entrepreneurial Behavior & Research, 19*(1), 53–71.

Häußler, S., & Ulrich, P. (2024). Exploring strategic corporate sustainability management in family businesses: A systematic literature review. *Review of Managerial Science*, 1–16.

He, Q., González-Cruz, T., Muñoz-de-Prat, J., & Montesinos-Sansaloni, E. (2025). Impact of founder controls on digital transformation: Evidence from listed family firms in China. *International Journal of Entrepreneurial Behavior & Research, 31*(6), 1476–1496.

Hernández-Linares, R., Kellermanns, F. W., López-Fernández, M. C., & Sarkar, S. (2020). The effect of socioemotional wealth on the relationship between entrepreneurial orientation and family business performance. *BRQ Business Research Quarterly, 23*(3), 174–192.

Jayantilal, S., Jorge, S. F., & Palacios, T. M. B. (2016). Effects of sibling competition on family firm succession: A game theory approach. *Journal of Family Business Strategy, 7*(4), 260–268.

Jayantilal, S., Palacios, T. B. B., & Jorge, S. F. (2015). Cultural dimension of Indian family firms–impact on successor selection. *Problems and Perspectives in Management, 13*(3), 96–103.

Jian, J., He, K., Liu, Y., & Sun, Y. (2024). Corporate social responsibility: Opportunistic behavior under earnings management? *Asia-Pacific Journal of Accounting & Economics, 31*(2), 247–268.

Jouber, H. (2024). Boardroom gender diversity and risk-taking in the insurance industry: Do organizational form and ownership structure matter? *Corporate Governance: The International Journal of Business in Society, 24*(2), 278–302.

Khidmat, W. B., Habib, M. D., Awan, S., & Raza, K. (2022). Female directors on corporate boards and their impact on corporate social responsibility (CSR): Evidence from China. *Management Research Review, 45*(4), 563–595.

Kraiczy, N. D., Hack, A., & Kellermanns, F. W. (2015). What makes a family firm innovative? CEO risk-taking propensity and the organizational context of family firms. *Journal of Product Innovation Management, 32*(3), 334–348.

Lee, K. S., Lim, G. H., & Lim, W. S. (2003). Family business succession: Appropriation risk and choice of successor. *Academy of Management Review, 28*(4), 657–666.

Li, W., Wang, Y., & Cao, L. (2023). Identities of the incumbent and the successor in the family business succession: Review and prospects. *Frontiers in Psychology, 14*, 1062829.

Liu, B., & Zhang, X. (2024). The impact of ESG and executive structure on the default risk of family businesses: Evidence from China. *Finance Research Letters, 61*, 104956.

Luo, X. R., Jeong, Y. C., & Chung, C. N. (2019). In the eye of the beholder: Global analysts' coverage of family firms in an emerging market. *Journal of Management, 45*(5), 1830–1857.

Ma, L. (2023). Corporate social responsibility reporting in family firms: Evidence from China. *Journal of Behavioral and Experimental Finance, 37*, 100730.

Martínez-Ferrero, J., Rodríguez-Ariza, L., & García-Sánchez, I. M. (2016). Corporate social responsibility as an entrenchment strategy, with a focus on the implications of family ownership. *Journal of Cleaner Production, 135*, 760–770.

Meier, O., & Thelisson, A. S. (2020). The succession dilemma in family firms: Case study of a French company. *Journal of Business Strategy, 42*(6), 406–411.

Oke, A., Turla, M., Osobajo, O., & Koutsoukos, S. (2025). Resolving the paradox of green innovation across generations in family firms: An exploratory analysis of incumbents and successors perceptions. *Journal of Family Business Management*. https://doi.org/10.1108/JFBM-03-2025-0068

Oussii, A. A., & Jeriji, M. (2025). Female directors' representation and firm carbon emissions performance: Does family control matter? *Journal of Family Business Management, 15*(3), 517–533.

Özbay, D., Adıgüzel, H., & Karahan Gökmen, M. (2023). Corporate social responsibility and tax avoidance: Channeling effect of family firms. *Journal of Corporate Accounting & Finance, 34*(3), 11–30.

Penney, C., Vardaman, J., Marler, L., & Antin-Yates, V. (2019). An image theory of strategic decision-making in family businesses. *Journal of Family Business Management, 9*(4), 451–467.

Putri, A. C., & Viverita, V. (2019). Risk preference of founder and descendant of Indonesian family firms. *Polish Journal of Management Studies, 20*.

Rasheed, M. S., Kouser, S., & Ling, Z. (2025). Corporate governance and stock price crash risk: Insights from an emerging market. *Asia-Pacific Financial Markets, 32*(2), 691–709.

Revilla, A. J., Perez-Luno, A., & Nieto, M. J. (2016). Does family involvement in management reduce the risk of business failure? The moderating role of entrepreneurial orientation. *Family Business Review, 29*(4), 365–379.

Rumanko, B., Lušňáková, Z., Moravanská, M., & Šajbidorová, M. (2021). Succession as a risk process in the survival of a family business—Case of Slovakia. *Journal of Risk and Financial Management, 14*(10), 458.

Saeed, A., Belghitar, Y., & Yousaf, A. (2016). Firm-level determinants of gender diversity in the boardrooms: Evidence from some emerging markets. *International Business Review, 25*(5), 1076–1088.

Salas-Paramo, J., & Escandon-Barbosa, D. (2025). Balancing growth and risk: How family firms shape value creation and avoid value loss over time. *Journal of Family Business Management*. https://doi.org/10.1108/jfbm-01-2025-0001

Samei, H., & Feyzbakhsh, A. (2015). Predecessors competency framework for nurturing successors in family firms. *International Journal of Entrepreneurial Behavior & Research, 21*(5), 731–752.

Saxena, A. (2013). Transgenerational succession in business groups in India. *Asia Pacific Journal of Management, 30*(3), 769–789.

Shen, N. (2018). Family business, transgenerational succession and diversification strategy: Implication from a dynamic socioemotional wealth model. *Cross Cultural & Strategic Management, 25*(4), 628–641.

Staehr, A. E. (2015). Human resource risk and succession planning: Implementing an integrated personal and financial consulting model in New York State. *Agricultural Finance Review, 75*(1), 133–139.

Sundaramurthy, C. (2008). Sustaining trust within family businesses. *Family Business Review, 21*(1), 89–102.

Syed, M. A., & Butt, S. A. (2017). Financial and non-financial determinants of corporate social responsibility: Empirical evidence from Pakistan. *Social Responsibility Journal, 13*(4), 780–797.

Szymczyk, K., & Włodarczyk, A. (2025). How to be green in highly turbulent business conditions? Evidence from family firms in Poland. *Journal of Family Business Management*. https://doi.org/10.1108/JFBM-12-2024-0289

Tan, Q., Guo, M., & Zhang, M. (2024). Family involvement in management and risk-taking of family firms: The moderating role of kinship composition. *Journal of Business Research, 182*, 114759.

Thevenard-Puthod, C. (2022). Hybrid succession teams: Understanding their formation and conditions for success. *Journal of Small Business Management, 60*(1), 178–218.

Vijayagopal, V., & Thenmozhi, M. (2025). Ownership dynamics and share pledging behavior in emerging markets: A zero-inflated model approach. *Cogent Economics & Finance, 13*(1), 2459182.

Wang, K., Huang, M., Zhang, L., & Dong, Q. (2024). Green innovation in family business succession: Exploring decision-making under parent-child co-governance. *Finance Research Letters, 67*, 105760.

Wu, S. W., Lin, F., & Wu, C. M. (2014). Corporate social responsibility and cost of capital: An empirical study of the Taiwan stock market. *Emerging Markets Finance and Trade, 50*(Suppl 1), 107–120.

Yang, M., Wang, Y., Bai, L., & Maresova, P. (2023). Corporate social responsibility, family involvement, and stock price crash risk. *Corporate social responsibility and environmental management, 30*(3), 1204–1225.

Yeh, Y. H. (2019). Corporate governance and family succession: New evidence from Taiwan. *Pacific-Basin Finance Journal, 57*, 100967.

Yeh, Y. H., & Liao, C. C. (2021). The impact of market and industry risk on family succession. *The North American Journal of Economics and Finance, 55*, 101021.

Zhang, Y., & Wei, X. (2025). Intergenerational succession and digital transformation in family firms: a socioemotional wealth perspective. *Cross Cultural & Strategic Management*.

Zheng, X., Zhu, B., & Yang, G. (2023). The soft landing: Does intrafamily succession matter for corporate risk-taking? *Pacific-Basin Finance Journal, 78*, 101967.

Zona, F., Pesci, C., & Zamarian, M. (2024). CEO risk preferences in family firms: Combining socioemotional wealth and gender identity perspectives. *Journal of Family Business Strategy, 15*(2), 100553.

# Chapter 8
# The Risk of ESG Controversies in Family Businesses: Governance and Ownership Determinants

**Abstract** This chapter examines the incidence of ESG controversies in family and non-family businesses, using OLS and 2SLS models on a sample of European listed companies from 2013 to 2022. The results show that the effects of governance and ownership structure variables on the propensity to engage in ESG controversies differ between family and non-family businesses. In family businesses, a higher share of family ownership significantly reduces the likelihood of controversies, while cultural diversity on the board increases the risk. Furthermore, board size and company profitability modulate exposure to ESG risk, suggesting that family governance arrangements can be both an asset and a vulnerability in preventing ESG conflicts. By focusing on ESG controversies as a specific manifestation of ESG risk, the chapter contributes to a research area that, as yet, does not constitute a consolidated thematic cluster in the bibliometric analysis presented in Chap. 2, thereby extending the literature on risk in family firms into a relatively underexplored domain.

**Keywords** ESG controversy · Risk · Family ownership · Board diversity

## 8.1 Research Motivations

ESG controversies, understood as adverse events or realized ESG performance failures that have become publicly visible in the environmental, social, or governance sphere, significantly compromise corporate performance, alter stakeholder perceptions, and generate harmful consequences in the short and long term, such as loss of market value, increased cost of capital, stock volatility, difficulty accessing financing, and legal penalties or compensation (Ab Aziz et al., 2025; Elamer & Boulhaga, 2024; Kim et al., 2025; Muhammad & Farooq, 2025; Samsudin et al., 2025). These impacts are particularly severe in regulated or environmentally sensitive sectors, where controversies can also increase systemic risks (Jucá et al., 2024; Gidage & Bhide, 2025). Companies involved in ESG controversies may engage in



A. M. Moisello, P. Gottardo, *Risk and Sustainability in Family Businesses*, SpringerBriefs in Finance, https://doi.org/10.1007/978-3-032-19995-9_8

opportunistic practices, such as ESG washing, which can erode investor trust (Fathoni et al., 2025), particularly among institutional investors active in Socially Responsible Investment funds (Alda, 2025). Furthermore, the effectiveness of corporate boards is a determining factor; the literature indicates that highly connected but overburdened boards of directors are less effective at monitoring and managing ESG risks, thereby increasing the likelihood of controversies (Shakri et al., 2025). In this context, governance plays a crucial role, and characteristics such as the presence of CSR committees, gender diversity, and sustainability-conscious leadership are mitigating mechanisms (Ab Aziz et al., 2025; Dutt et al., 2025; Samsudin et al., 2025).

For family businesses, avoiding ESG controversies is essential not only for reputational reasons but also to safeguard the socioemotional wealth on which their identity and continuity are based (Berrone et al., 2012). The literature indicates that family firms tend to be more protective of their long-term reputation; however, this orientation can lead to defensive behavior and reduced openness to the needs of external stakeholders, resulting in adverse effects on ESG performance (Nimer et al., 2025). However, more mature family businesses demonstrate a greater ability to adapt to sustainability logic, developing more sophisticated and inclusive governance structures that can mitigate ESG risks over time (Nimer et al., 2025). Furthermore, the centrality of family interests, if not balanced, can hinder innovation and transparency, thereby increasing vulnerability to controversy (Ng & Hamilton, 2024). On the other hand, when family firms adopt sound ESG practices and responsibly disclose their sustainability activities, they can benefit from tangible advantages, such as lower debt costs, owing to greater trust among creditors (Sari et al., 2024). Avoiding ESG controversies, therefore, allows family businesses to strengthen their strategic resilience, increase stakeholder confidence, and ensure generational continuity in line with the expectations of an increasingly sustainability-conscious society. We know that ESG adoption is often seen by family businesses not only as a regulatory obligation but as a strategic lever to reduce reputational and financial risk (Hughes et al., 2025). Moreover, recent evidence confirms that firms with stronger ESG performance are less exposed to default risk (Liu & Zhang, 2024). However, we still lack a systematic understanding of what drives explicitly ESG risk in family firms, that is, the likelihood at the firm level of the occurrence and detection of such events, conditional on governance and ownership characteristics. In particular, existing research has not yet clarified how family-specific governance traits, such as ownership concentration or board composition, impact the likelihood of ESG controversies. Given these considerations, it is essential to investigate how governance characteristics influence exposure to ESG controversies in family businesses relative to non-family businesses and within family businesses.

We built a database for the period 2013–2022 by cross-referencing data on ESG controversy scores from the Refinitiv Eikon database with data on corporate governance indicators relating to board composition and size and corporate ownership structure, controlling for company size, the performance and environmental sensitivity of the sector to which they belong. Data taken in part from Orbis Bureau Van Dick, in part from Refinitiv Eikon, and part hand collected from firms' corporate governance reports. The database enabled us to perform descriptive statistics and both OLS and 2SLS regression analyses to assess, on the one hand, differences between family and non-family businesses in these respects, and, on the other, to verify the links between governance characteristics and exposure to ESG controversies, highlighting sources of heterogeneity within family businesses.

## 8.2 Literature Review and Development of Hypotheses

The presence of family in the ownership and strategic control of the company introduces a management logic strongly influenced by non-economic objectives, including reputation, generational continuity, and community ties (Berrone et al., 2012). Socioemotional Wealth perspective (SEW) offers a valuable interpretive framework for understanding this orientation. Families are motivated to preserve their socioemotional capital, which includes social recognition, family influence, and collective identity (Gómez-Mejía et al., 2007; Le Breton-Miller et al., 2011). In this context, ESG controversies represent a threat to the external legitimacy and symbolic continuity of the entrepreneurial family and its values.

Recent studies indicate that family businesses are highly cautious about decisions that could compromise their image among stakeholders. Concern for reputation leads family firms to engage more in CSR initiatives to mitigate reputational risk (Rodríguez-Ariza et al., 2017). Furthermore, Legitimacy Theory suggests that perceived legitimacy by society is a crucial resource for the long-term survival of businesses, and family firms, which are often integrated into the local social fabric, are incentivized to align themselves with the normative and cultural expectations of stakeholders (Suchman, 1995; Chou et al., 2016).

Ng and Hamilton (2024) reinforce this view, demonstrating that family businesses that are firmly focused on SEW are less likely to innovate but more anchored in reputational and survival logics, favoring incremental and prudent strategies. This suggests that, although less dynamic, such businesses are also less prone to strategic deviations that could conflict with ESG values.

Similarly, Sari et al. (2024) demonstrate how family ownership positively moderates the relationship between CSR disclosure and debt cost. Family firms, which are more reputation-conscious, utilize CSR reporting as a signal of reliability to creditors, thereby avoiding opaque or risky behavior. Nimer et al. (2025) observe that although family ownership initially has a negative effect on ESG performance in emerging contexts, this tendency diminishes as the company matures, suggesting that the SEW logic evolves toward more proactive forms of legitimization.

Finally, Diéguez-Soto et al. (2024) confirm that the presence of family in the business fosters greater attention to the long-term implications of strategic choices, highlighting that family businesses are more cautious and focused on values and reputation. A strong family presence in ownership reinforces identification between the family and the business, making the company's reputation a direct reflection of the family's identity. In this context, ESG controversies not only threaten the legitimacy of the company but also the family's symbolic capital, amplifying sensitivity to reputational risk (Gavana et al., 2017).

H1. *In family businesses, greater concentration of ownership in the hands of the family is negatively associated with the propensity to engage in ESG controversies.*

In the context of growing regulatory and social expectations regarding environmental, social, and governance (ESG) responsibilities, companies are increasingly exposed to the risk of ESG controversies (Kim & Lyon, 2015). Such controversies are episodes in which a company is perceived as failing to comply with socially expected standards of sustainability and transparency, resulting in negative impacts on its reputation, market value, and institutional legitimacy (Sassen et al., 2016). Consequently, the composition of the board of directors is a key factor in preventing such situations, serving as a channel for strategic responses to environmental and regulatory pressures (Muhammad & Farooq, 2025).

According to Legitimacy Theory (Suchman, 1995), organizations strive to obtain and maintain social approval by aligning their behaviors with shared values. Misalignment, as in the case of inadequate ESG behaviors, can lead to a loss of legitimacy and subsequent reputational and regulatory pressures (Dowling & Pfeffer, 1975; Deegan, 2002). Board demographic diversity, understood as a heterogeneous composition with respect to gender and culture, can strengthen perceived legitimacy by promoting more transparent and inclusive governance that aligns with institutional expectations (Yilmaz et al., 2023).

Board cultural diversity broadens the regulatory and value perspectives represented on the board, promoting a greater understanding of ESG pressures in international contexts and enhancing the ability to adapt to different standards (Khan et al., 2019; Cheung & Lai, 2023). It stimulates a stronger focus on social and environmental reporting, thanks to the heterogeneity of views and the enrichment of the decision-making process (Gallego-Álvarez and Pucheta-Martínez, 2022a). Cultural diversity within the board of directors can strengthen the company's ability to anticipate emerging institutional expectations, serving as a strategic information channel and promoting proactive behavior on sustainability, thereby reducing the risk of ESG controversies (Padungsaksawasdi & Treepongkaruna, 2024).

At the same time, gender diversity has been shown to have a significant impact in promoting an ethical and sustainable approach to governance. Women in board positions are associated with a greater aversion to reputational risk, greater attention to ESG issues, and a greater propensity to enhance transparency (Post & Byron, 2015; Muttakin et al., 2015). Recent studies have also shown that women on boards contribute to improving CSR commitment even in family businesses, mitigating opaque or aggressive practices (Seckin-Halac et al., 2021; Sial et al., 2019). In particular, female family leaders appear more inclined to protect the company's external legitimacy, precisely because they are closely tied to family identity and reputation (Song et al., 2025).

In family businesses, organizational legitimacy is strongly influenced by the pursuit of socioemotional wealth (Gómez-Mejía et al., 2011). The protection of family reputation, socio-political control, and intergenerational identity leads these companies to adopt defensive and selective ESG communication strategies (Rodríguez-Ariza et al., 2017). However, such behaviors can result in high exposure to ESG controversy risk, especially in contexts where regulatory and social pressure is intense (Katmon et al., 2019).

Specific configurations, such as the presence of a female chair of the board, are associated with improved ESG performance, particularly in the social and governance dimensions. Family businesses led by women exhibit greater ESG regulatory compliance than those led by men, suggesting the critical importance of leadership and board composition in these contexts (Wang & Wang, 2024). The presence of culturally and gender-diverse board members introduces discontinuity into endogamous decision-making processes, promoting openness to the external environment and sensitivity to issues of legitimacy (Paolone et al., 2024).

Demographic diversity enhances monitoring, enriches decision-making, and contributes to a more inclusive and pluralistic representation of stakeholders. Therefore, we expect that the integration of gender and cultural diversity on the boards of family businesses will serve as a strategic lever for strengthening the business's resilience to institutional legitimacy pressures and mitigating the risk of ESG controversies. We posit the following research hypothesis:

H2. *In family businesses, demographic diversity on the board of directors, in terms of gender and cultural diversity, is negatively associated with the propensity to engage in ESG controversies.*

## 8.3 Data and Research Methodology

The database used to verify the above research hypotheses consists of non-financial companies listed in 16 European Union countries from 2013 to 2022. The 16 European Union countries included are: Austria, Belgium, Cyprus, Finland, France, Germany, Greece, Ireland, Italy, Luxembourg, Malta, the Netherlands, Poland, Portugal, Spain, and Hungary. The initial sample consists of non-financial listed firms for which the ESG Controversies Score is available in the Refinitiv Eikon database and the governance data in the Orbis database for this period. Some EU countries (e.g., Czech Republic and certain CEE markets) were not included because there are too few listed non-financial firms with continuous ESG controversies coverage over the sample period or because coverage of board and ownership data was inconsistent. The final sample, after excluding observations with missing explanatory variable data, comprises a panel of 3820 observations. Of the total sample, 2513 observations (65.79%) relate to non-family businesses, while the remaining 1307 observations (34.21%) relate to family businesses. To distinguish between family and non-family businesses, we applied an approach based on business ownership, assuming that a business can be considered family-owned if one or more members of the same family own 20% or more of the outstanding voting shares issued by the business (Villalonga & Amit, 2010). Ownership data are drawn from the Bureau van Dijk Orbis database, using the ultimate ownership and direct shareholders modules, and we identify family shareholders based on surnames, family business group information, and manual checks of annual reports and corporate governance reports. The family vs non-family classification is updated on a yearly basis for each firm-year in our panel (2013–2022).

We used the annual global score from the Refinitiv Eikon database as a proxy for ESG controversies. The score assigned ranges from 0 to 100. If a company's score in a given year is 100, the probability that the company will encounter ESG controversies is minimal; the probability increases as the score decreases.

Among the explanatory variables used in the subsequent models, FO takes into account the weight of the family in the company's ownership structure, measured in terms of the percentage of all voting shares held by family members (source: Bureau van Dijk Orbis and manual checks) (Dal Maso et al., 2020). BS quantifies the size of the board, that is, the total number of board members (Coles et al., 2008), while FB measures the weight of the presence of members of a family on the board as the ratio between family members and the total number of board members (Greco et al., 2014; López-González et al., 2019). Although FB is primarily intended to capture the degree of direct family influence within family-controlled firms, it also retains empirical significance when applied to non-family-controlled firms. This is because former family-controlled firms may continue to include family members on the board of directors even after relinquishing ownership control, as representatives of minority shareholders (González et al., 2013). BGD considers the gender composition of the board by measuring the ratio of women to total board members (Cruz et al., 2019; Li et al., 2017; Naciti, 2019; Nadeem et al., 2020). BCD measures cultural differences among board members, taking into account each member's nationality relative to the country in which the company is registered (Gallego-Álvarez & Pucheta-Martínez, 2022b; Zaid et al., 2020). Board information (composition and nationality of board members) has been hand-collected from a firm's corporate governance reports.

As additional control variables, we used company size, measured as the natural logarithm of total assets (S) (source: Bureau van Dijk Orbis), a measure of financial performance given by ROA (source: Bureau van Dijk Orbis), and a dummy variable for environmental sensitivity defined based on the company's sector (ES). Environmental sensitivity (Branco & Rodrigues, 2008) is represented by a binary variable equal to 1 for firms operating in industries with elevated ecological risk, and 0 for those in less exposed sectors. Finally, since companies with a stronger focus on innovation show greater attention to reputational risks and different exposure to ESG controversies (Duong & Huang, 2025), we also controlled for the annual amount of research and development expenditure incurred by companies in relation to total assets (R&D) (source: Bureau van Dijk Orbis).

To verify whether governance characteristics affect the exposure of family and non-family businesses to ESG controversies, we employed two models with two estimation methods. The first model estimates the relationship between the ESG controversies score and the explanatory variables indicated above, excluding research and development expenditure. The second model estimates the same relationship, including this variable among the control variables. In both models, we perform separate analyses for non-family and family businesses. The basic versions of the two models are estimated using OLS regression. To verify the robustness of the results, the models are re-estimated using a 2SLS approach, with the lagged explanatory variables serving as instruments. We use lagged governance variables as instruments to mitigate the possibility of reverse causality between controversies and governance changes. Both models include dummies to control industry (I), country (C) and year fixed effects (T).

$$\begin{aligned} ESG\,controversies_{it} = {} & \alpha_0 + \beta_1 \mathrm{bs} + \beta_2 \mathrm{fb} + \beta_3 \mathrm{fown} + \beta_4 \mathrm{bgd} \\ & + \beta_5 \mathrm{bcd} + \beta_6 \mathrm{s} + \beta_7 \mathrm{roa} + \beta_8 \mathrm{es} + \sum_{n=9}^{N1} \beta_n I_{n,it} \\ & + \sum_{m=1}^{M1} \beta_m C_{m,it} + \sum_{p=1}^{10} \beta_p T_{p,it} \end{aligned} \tag{8.1}$$

$$\begin{aligned} ESG\,controversies_{it} = {} & \alpha_0 + \beta_1 \mathrm{bs} + \beta_2 \mathrm{fb} + \beta_3 \mathrm{fown} + \beta_4 \mathrm{bgd} \\ & + \beta_5 \mathrm{bcd} + \beta_6 \mathrm{s} + \beta_7 \mathrm{roa} + \beta_8 \mathrm{es} + \beta_9 \mathrm{r\,\&\,d} \\ & + \sum_{n=9}^{N1} \beta_n I_{n,it} + \sum_{m=1}^{M1} \beta_m C_{m,it} + \sum_{p=1}^{10} \beta_p T_{p,it} \end{aligned} \tag{8.2}$$

The baseline specification in model (8.1) without r&d allows us to retain a larger number of observations, given missing r&d data for almost 52% of the sample firm-years. The extended model (8.2) includes r&d as a control, following prior work that links innovation intensity to ESG behavior and controversies (e.g., Duong & Huang, 2025).

## 8.4 Results and Discussion

Table 8.1 in panel A shows the descriptive statistics for the ESG controversies score and the explanatory variables. The average controversy score for the companies in the sample is approximately 0.9, indicating that the probability of a listed company in our sample encountering an ESG controversy is moderate. However, the sample exhibits considerable volatility (standard deviation = 0.23), with a maximum score of 1 and a minimum of 0.008. The results of the descriptive analysis also show that the propensity to have ESG controversies in family and non-family businesses is not statistically significant. While the average score for non-family businesses is 0.902, that for family businesses is 0.909; however, the difference is not significant (t = −0.91). From the perspective of governance characteristics, however, there are significant differences between non-family businesses and family businesses. All the explanatory variables considered have statistically different mean values at a significance level of 1% for the samples of non-family and family businesses. This

**Table 8.1** Descriptive statistics

| Panel A[a] | | | | | | | | | T-test |
|---|---|---|---|---|---|---|---|---|---|
| Descriptive statistics | Full sample | | | | Non-family firms | | Family firms | | |
| Variable | Mean | Std dev | Min | Max | Mean | Std dev | Mean | Std dev | |
| esgcontr | 0.904 | 0.230 | 0.00806 | 1 | 0.902 | 0.232 | 0.909 | 0.227 | −0.91 |
| bsize | 8.649 | 3.763 | 2 | 24 | 8.718 | 3.892 | 8.550 | 3.567 | 2.24 ** |
| fboard | 0.107 | 0.176 | 0 | 1 | 0.007 | 0.039 | 0.249 | 0.197 | −78.98 *** |
| fown | 0.230 | 0.296 | 0 | 1 | 0.008 | 0.032 | 0.549 | 0.199 | −175.43 *** |
| bgd | 0.278 | 0.156 | 0 | 0.8 | 0.265 | 0.157 | 0.297 | 0.153 | −10.44 *** |
| bcd | 0.174 | 0.236 | 0 | 1 | 0.208 | 0.249 | 0.125 | 0.207 | 18.45 *** |
| size | 13.495 | 2.156 | 7.074 | 20.086 | 13.666 | 2.239 | 13.251 | 2.005 | 9.86 *** |
| roa | 0.021 | 0.103 | −0.99 | 0.871 | 0.015 | 0.117 | 0.030 | 0.078 | −7.93 *** |
| envses | 0.169 | 0.374 | 0 | 1 | 0.188 | 0.390 | 0.141 | 0.348 | 6.34 *** |
| r&d | 0.041 | 0.063 | 0.000 | 0.615 | 0.046 | 0.071 | 0.031 | 0.043 | 8.16 *** |
| | | | Panel B | | | | | | |
| Country | Observations | Percent | Years | Observations | Percent | | | | |
| Austria | 117 | 3.06 | 2013 | 250 | 6.54 | | | | |
| Belgium | 235 | 6.15 | 2014 | 289 | 7.57 | | | | |
| Cyprus | 11 | 0.29 | 2015 | 300 | 7.85 | | | | |
| Finland | 287 | 7.51 | 2016 | 313 | 8.19 | | | | |
| France | 702 | 18.38 | 2017 | 333 | 8.72 | | | | |
| Germany | 830 | 21.73 | 2018 | 360 | 9.42 | | | | |
| Greece | 114 | 2.98 | 2019 | 369 | 9.66 | | | | |
| Ireland | 167 | 4.37 | 2020 | 462 | 12.10 | | | | |
| Italy | 323 | 8.46 | 2021 | 586 | 15.34 | | | | |
| Luxembourg | 103 | 2.70 | 2022 | 558 | 14.61 | | | | |
| Malta | 15 | 0.39 | | | | | | | |

| | | | | | | | | | |
|---|---|---|---|---|---|---|---|---|---|
| Netherlands | 341 | 8.93 | | | | | | | |
| Poland | 143 | 3.74 | | | | | | | |
| Portugal | 68 | 1.78 | | | | | | | |
| Spain | 348 | 9.11 | | | | | | | |
| Hungary | 16 | 0.42 | | | | | | | |
| Total | 3820 | 100.00 | | 3820 | 100.00 | | | | |

[a]Note. This table presents descriptive statistics (mean and standard deviation) for the ESG controversies score and the other variables used in this study. The sample contains 3820 firm-year observations (2513 non-family and 1307 family firm obs) for the period 2013–2022. The independent variables are board gender diversity (bgd), board size (bsize), board cultural diversity (bcd), family ownership (fown), family members on board (fboard), firm dimension (size), profitability (roa), environmental sensitivity (envses) and research and development expenditure (r&d). T-test reports the t-statistics and the significance of the difference in the mean for each variable between the non-family and family sub-samples. Significance: **$p<.05$ level, ***$p<.01$ level

result is expected for those characteristics that distinguish the two categories of companies, such as the presence of family members on the board or cultural diversity among board members. Family and non-family firms differ in the concentration of ownership in the hands of individuals linked by family ties, the weight of research and development expenses, and even the size of the companies. What is most relevant, however, is that the differences between family-owned and non-family-owned listed companies are more pervasive than this, affecting various aspects, including board size, gender diversity on boards, financial performance, and even the choice of sector in which to operate. These aspects demonstrate that non-family and family businesses are significantly different. The question we ask at this point is whether these differences also affect the extent to which companies are involved in ESG controversies and the attitudes toward them. Panel B of Table 8.1 shows the breakdown of the sample observations by country, and their temporal distribution. Distribution by country shows a prevalence of ESG controversies coverage in Germany, France, Italy, Netherlands, Spain and Finland, but this reflects country and stock market sizes. The temporal distribution of observations is relatively uniform from 2013 to 2022, with a gradual increase in recent years attributable to improved coverage of ESG controversy reports.

Table 8.2 presents Pearson correlation coefficients for the entire sample between the ESG controversies score and the variables measuring the companies' governance characteristics. The correlation coefficients between the variables are low or moderate. The highest correlation coefficient for the dependent variable is that between the ESG controversies score and company size. The value is negative (−0.425), indicating a strong inverse relationship between company size and the likelihood of being involved in an ESG controversy. Among the governance characteristics considered, the highest correlation coefficient is between company size, measured by the natural logarithm of its assets, and board size. As expected, the

**Table 8.2** Pearson correlation coefficients

| Variables | bsize | fboard | fown | bgd | bcd | size | roa | envses | r&d |
|---|---|---|---|---|---|---|---|---|---|
| esgcontr | **−0.280** | **0.078** | 0.028 | **−0.103** | **−0.040** | **−0.425** | **0.042** | **−0.091** | **0.099** |
| bsize | | **−0.142** | **−0.044** | **0.181** | 0.012 | **0.638** | **0.076** | **0.125** | **−0.185** |
| fboard | | | **0.708** | **0.094** | **−0.225** | **−0.230** | **0.039** | **−0.052** | **−0.075** |
| fown | | | | **0.093** | **−0.189** | **−0.126** | **0.067** | **−0.079** | **−0.117** |
| bgd | | | | | **−0.086** | **0.141** | **0.029** | **−0.068** | −0.030 |
| bcd | | | | | | **0.254** | −0.010 | −0.009 | **0.082** |
| size | | | | | | | **0.171** | **0.170** | **−0.316** |
| roa | | | | | | | | −0.017 | **−0.381** |
| envses | | | | | | | | | **−0.223** |

Note. This table presents the descriptive statistics (Pearson correlations) for the ESG controversies score and the other variables used in this study. The sample contains 3820 firm-year observations for the period 2013–2022. The independent variables are board gender diversity (bgd), board size (bsize), board cultural diversity (bcd), family ownership (fown), family members on board (fboard), firm dimension (size), profitability (roa), environmental sensitivity (envses), and research and development expenditure (r&d). Significance: bold coefficients. $p<.05$ level value is positive, 0.638, indicating a clear direct relationship between the two variables. However, beyond these two coefficients, the others take on more modest values. We have highlighted in bold those that are statistically significant at a 5% confidence level, indicating the absence of pathological situations and, therefore, of multicollinearity effects between the explanatory variables, which could invalidate subsequent analyses. The calculation and analysis of the variance inflation factors in the subsequent regression models, whose values are shown next to each estimated coefficient in Panel A of Table 8.3, confirm the evidence inferable from the correlation table: none of the coefficients take on high values. There are only a couple of values greater than two relating to the size and board size variables in model (8.2). This indicates that none of the explanatory variables are strongly correlated with the others, so the effect on the standard errors of the estimates is modest and the effects of the correlations between the explanatory variables are not capable of compromising the stability of the models.

However, notable differences emerge in the effects of governance characteristics on ESG controversies across the two types of companies.

Table 8.3 presents the results of estimating models (8.1) and (8.2). Panel A displays the OLS estimates for the two models, while Panel B presents the 2SLS results using lagged explanatory variables as instruments.

The results indicate a difference between family-controlled and non-family-controlled companies in the effect of family ownership on the propensity to be involved in ESG controversies. In family-controlled companies, higher family shareholding is associated with a lower probability of ESG controversies, with an estimated coefficient of 0.074 in the 2SLS model, statistically significant at the 5% level. This result supports H1 and is consistent with the literature on socioemotional wealth (Gómez-Mejía et al., 2007), which suggests that controlling families tend to prioritize reputation, family identity, and intergenerational continuity, adopting behaviors that are more attentive to the ethical, social, and environmental implications of their business decisions. In this context, family ownership provides a means of exercising direct and responsible control over the company, thereby reducing potential conflicts with external stakeholders (Berrone et al., 2010).

Conversely, in non-family-controlled companies, family shareholding is associated with a higher incidence of ESG controversies, with a coefficient of −0.470 in the 2SLS model (8.1), which is statistically significant at the 1% level. This result can be interpreted in light of a possible misalignment between ownership and control: the family retains a share of the capital but no longer exercises significant influence over governance and strategic decisions. This may be the case for former family businesses that have lost control following the sale of shares, while retaining a shareholding (Miller et al., 2011). This condition of "ownership without control" can generate latent tensions between family interests and those of the new governance, particularly in areas of high value, such as ESG policies. The family, deprived of the ability to influence corporate conduct directly, may respond in oppositional or conflictual ways to management decisions, thereby increasing controversies (Chrisman et al., 2005).

**Table 8.3** ESG controversies and governance characteristics: OLS regression models

| | All firms | | | | | | Non-family firms | | | | | | Family firms | | | | | |
|---|---|---|---|---|---|---|---|---|---|---|---|---|---|---|---|---|---|---|
| | Model (8.1) | | | Model (8.2) | | | Model (8.1) | | | Model (8.2) | | | Model (8.1) | | | Model (8.2) | | |
| *Panel A* | | | | | | | | | | | | | | | | | | |
| | **Coeff** | **Std err** | **VIF** | **Coeff** | **Std err** | **VIF** | **Coeff** | **Std err** | **VIF** | **Coeff** | **Std err** | **VIF** | **Coeff** | **Std err** | **VIF** | **Coeff** | **Std err** | **VIF** |
| Intercept | 1.907 | 0.028*** | | 2.116 | 0.048*** | | 1.864 | 0.034*** | | 2.074 | 0.059*** | | 1.921 | 0.054*** | | 2.103 | 0.090*** | |
| bsize | −0.004 | 0.001*** | 2.02 | −0.002 | 0.001 | 2.48 | −0.003 | 0.001*** | 2.06 | −0.001 | 0.002 | 2.50 | -0.008 | 0.001*** | 2.25 | -0.006 | 0.002** | 3.24 |
| fboard | 0.023 | 0.029 | 2.1 | −0.027 | 0.050 | 1.95 | 0.044 | 0.101 | 1.77 | 0.600 | 0.175*** | 1.98 | -0.010 | 0.033 | 1.59 | -0.019 | 0.062 | 1.97 |
| fown | −0.001 | 0.013 | 1.93 | 0.020 | 0.020 | 1.77 | −0.456 | 0.110*** | 1.82 | −1.032 | 0.166*** | 2.03 | 0.054 | 0.026** | 1.3 | 0.042 | 0.045 | 1.62 |
| bgd | −0.008 | 0.021 | 1.69 | 0.099 | 0.035*** | 1.65 | 0.035 | 0.027 | 1.71 | 0.137 | 0.044*** | 1.62 | -0.055 | 0.035 | 1.80 | 0.084 | 0.062 | 2.16 |
| bcd | 0.008 | 0.012 | 1.55 | 0.023 | 0.028 | 1.99 | 0.019 | 0.014 | 1.45 | 0.057 | 0.024** | 1.87 | -0.038 | 0.022* | 1.95 | -0.097 | 0.040** | 2.68 |
| size | −0.061 | 0.002*** | 1.98 | −0.080 | 0.003*** | 2.66 | −0.059 | 0.002*** | 2.05 | −0.082 | 0.004*** | 2.8 | -0.061 | 0.004*** | 2.25 | -0.067 | 0.006*** | 3.20 |
| envses | 0.030 | 0.007*** | 1.59 | 0.038 | 0.010*** | 1.42 | 0.045 | 0.009*** | 1.82 | 0.050 | 0.012*** | 1.47 | 0.013 | 0.011 | 1.54 | 0.000 | 0.017 | 1.74 |
| roa | 0.194 | 0.029*** | 1.09 | 0.163 | 0.041*** | 1.29 | 0.212 | 0.033*** | 1.11 | 0.215 | 0.050*** | 1.46 | 0.069 | 0.059 | 1.13 | -0.020 | 0.084 | 1.15 |
| r&d | | | | −0.273 | 0.092*** | 1.60 | | | | −0.328 | 0.106*** | 1.76 | | | | 0.108 | 0.209 | 1.46 |
| Industry | Yes | | | Yes | | | Yes | | | Yes | | | Yes | | | Yes | | |
| Country | Yes | | | Yes | | | Yes | | | Yes | | | Yes | | | Yes | | |
| Years | Yes | | | Yes | | | Yes | | | Yes | | | Yes | | | Yes | | |
| Adj. R-squared | 0.233 | | | 0.289 | | | 0.230 | | | 0.291 | | | 0.270 | | | 0.337 | | |

*Panel B*

| | Coeff | Std err | Coeff | Std err | Coeff | Std err | Coeff | Std err | Coeff | Std err | Coeff | Std err |
|---|---|---|---|---|---|---|---|---|---|---|---|---|
| Intercept | 1.912 | 0.028*** | 2.154 | 0.051*** | 1.879 | 0.034*** | 2.103 | 0.062*** | 1.925 | 0.053*** | 2.222 | 0.092 *** |
| bsize | −0.002 | 0.001*** | 0.002 | 0.001 | −0.002 | 0.001* | 0.002 | 0.002 | −0.006 | 0.001*** | −0.002 | 0.002 |
| fboard | 0.048 | 0.028* | 0.025 | 0.049 | 0.099 | 0.101 | 0.726 | 0.179*** | 0.030 | 0.031 | 0.059 | 0.054 |
| fown | −0.004 | 0.013 | 0.011 | 0.020 | −0.470 | 0.109*** | −1.135 | 0.169*** | 0.074 | 0.025*** | 0.070 | 0.045 |
| bgd | 0.031 | 0.020 | 0.100 | 0.035*** | 0.060 | 0.026** | 0.137 | 0.047*** | −0.017 | 0.033 | 0.051 | 0.057 |
| bcd | 0.015 | 0.011 | 0.027 | 0.018 | 0.040 | 0.013*** | 0.072 | 0.022*** | −0.042 | 0.020** | −0.060 | 0.036* |
| size | −0.063 | 0.002*** | −0.083 | 0.003*** | −0.062 | 0.002*** | −0.085 | 0.004*** | −0.063 | 0.003*** | −0.076 | 0.006*** |
| envses | 0.029 | 0.007*** | 0.033 | 0.010*** | 0.047 | 0.009*** | 0.043 | 0.013*** | 0.003 | 0.011 | 0.006 | 0.016 |
| roa | 0.272 | 0.054*** | 0.257 | 0.078*** | 0.333 | 0.064*** | 0.350 | 0.105*** | 0.001 | 0.111 | −0.159 | 0.145 |
| r&d | | | −0.265 | 0.112** | | | −0.286 | 0.145** | | | 0.054 | 0.224 |
| Industry | Yes | | Yes | | Yes | | Yes | | Yes | | Yes | |
| Country | Yes | | Yes | | Yes | | Yes | | Yes | | Yes | |
| Years | Yes | | Yes | | Yes | | Yes | | Yes | | Yes | |
| Adj. R-squared | 0.226 | | 0.277 | | 0.223 | | 0.277 | | 0.259 | | 0.328 | |

Note. This table presents Panel A—ordinary least squares (OLS) and Panel B—two-stage least squares (2SLS) results based on our models (8.1) and (8.2). The sample contains 3820 firm-year observations (2513 non-family and 1307 family firm obs) for the period 2013–2022. The dependent variable is the ESG controversies score, the independent variables are board gender diversity (bgd), board size (bsize), board cultural diversity (bcd), family ownership (fown), family members on board (fboard), firm dimension (size), profitability (roa), environmental sensitivity (envses), research and development expenditure (r&d), and Industry, Country, and Year dummies. Significance: **p<.05 level, ***p<.01 level

Therefore, the role of the family as a shareholder has opposite effects depending on whether or not it retains control of the company, suggesting that it is not the mere presence of family ownership that determines responsible ESG behavior, but rather the possibility of exercising an active influence consistent with family values (Gómez-Mejía et al., 2011).

A second finding is the amplifying effect of board size on the propensity for ESG controversies in family businesses. The variable has an estimated coefficient of −0.006 in the 2SLS model, which is statistically significant at the 1% level. In family businesses, a larger board may entail risks of decision-making inefficiency and communication problems (Wang et al., 2013), which can hinder the consistent management of ESG practices. Furthermore, family businesses tend to favor quick decision-making and cohesive control, which are better supported by smaller boards (Che & Langli, 2015). The effect of board size in the two models for the sample of non-family businesses is weaker, regardless of the estimation method used.

Empirical evidence confirms that larger boards can reduce ESG controversies, but only in the presence of effective governance structures (Treepongkaruna et al., 2024). On the other hand, smaller boards in concentrated ownership firms allow for greater alignment between ownership and control, more efficient governance, and less complexity in decision-making processes, which can foster a more consistent and responsive approach to ESG management (Gupta & Chauhan, 2023).

In closing, it is important to note that board size is positively associated with a company's reputation (da Costa et al., 2023). Larger companies require more complex governance structures to manage operational and legal complexities. Companies that are more visible—in terms of size, media presence, or institutional exposure—are subject to more intense public scrutiny and greater pressure from external stakeholders, the media, regulatory authorities, and civil society (Gavana et al., 2017). This exposure amplifies the likelihood that any behavior inconsistent with environmental, social, or governance expectations will be identified, reported, and turned into controversy (Boulton, 2024). Furthermore, public attention also gives greater resonance to minor violations, making companies more exposed to the so-called penalty of prominence (Zavyalova et al., 2012). Our results show that company size has an amplifying effect on ESG controversies for both family businesses (coefficient estimated in the 2SLS model equal to −0.063, statistically significant at 1%) and non-family businesses (coefficient estimated in the (8.1) 2SLS equal to −0.062, statistically significant at 1%). From this perspective, visibility is therefore not only a competitive advantage or a relational resource, but also a potential liability of legitimacy, requiring more sophisticated reputation management strategies to prevent and mitigate ESG risks.

The results indicate that cultural diversity on the board of directors tends to increase the likelihood of ESG controversies in family businesses (with an estimated coefficient in the (8.1) 2SLS model of −0.042, statistically significant at the 5% level), and the effect of board gender diversity is not significant, thus not supporting H2. The effect of board cultural diversity can be explained by several mechanisms recognized in the literature. First, the presence of board members with different cultural backgrounds can lead to divergent values and priorities, which do not always align with the company's ESG objectives. In family contexts, where traditional values and a homogeneous view of governance often prevail, such misalignments can be amplified, generating internal tensions and inconsistent decisions on sustainability (Cacciotti & Ucbasaran, 2018).

Secondly, culturally diverse boards face greater complexity in decision-making processes, with increased difficulty in building consensus and responding promptly to ESG issues. This is particularly relevant in family businesses, where the lack of structured processes can exacerbate the challenge of overcoming cultural barriers in governance (Ponomareva et al., 2022).

Another factor is the differing interpretations of ESG priorities among board members, influenced by their cultural backgrounds. This can lead to inconsistent or contradictory ESG practices, thereby increasing the likelihood of external scrutiny and criticism from stakeholders and heightening controversy (DasGupta, 2025).

Furthermore, studies on gender and ethnic diversity on boards highlight contrasting effects on ESG performance. Although diversity can introduce new perspectives and stimulate innovation, it can also generate friction in decision-making if not managed effectively, especially in family businesses, where conservative values may conflict with more progressive approaches to ESG (Anand et al., 2025). However, the results from our two model estimates suggest that gender diversity does not have a substantial effect on the propensity to engage in ESG controversies among family businesses, once other explanatory variables are controlled for. For non-family businesses, the results suggest that higher board gender diversity reduces the likelihood of incurring ESG controversies.

Finally, the results show a negative relationship between corporate profitability and ESG controversies for non-family firms, with a coefficient of 0.414 in the 2SLS model (8.1), statistically significant at the 1% level. This suggests that more profitable companies are better positioned to prevent ESG controversies, likely due to greater financial slack that enables investment in compliance, stakeholder engagement, and sustainability programs (Tan & Tuluca, 2024). Profitability may also support a strategic view of ESG, in which high-performing firms regard sustainability as a long-term value driver rather than a cost. For instance, Dsouza et al. (2025) demonstrate that ESG integration enhances market valuation and operational capacity, particularly in high-performance firms that incorporate sustainability into their strategic planning. Interestingly, this inverse relationship is not observed among family firms. Yet, this finding aligns with the idea that profitable companies are generally better able to engage in ESG. Notably, the average ROA among family firms in our sample is twice that of non-family firms (3% vs. 1.5%), a difference that is statistically significant at the 1% level ($t = 9.73$) and is accompanied by lower profitability volatility (standard deviation of 0.078 for family firms vs. 0.117 for non-family firms). This evidence suggests that family businesses, even if more profitable than non-family firms, may utilize fewer financial resources to prevent ESG controversies or may not allocate these resources efficiently.

The differences between OLS and 2SLS estimates arise because the 2SLS procedure corrects for some potential endogeneity problems that affect OLS estimates, in particular reverse causality between ESG controversies and governance adjustments, which may be especially relevant for profitability and size. The differences between model (8.1) and model (8.2) that takes into account research and development expenditure are mainly driven by sample composition, that is, the loss of observations when r&d is missing, and by the fact that r&d absorbs part of the variance associated with innovation-driven ESG strategies. We also note that the main coefficients of interest (family ownership, board size, board diversity) are qualitatively stable across the models with and without r&d.

The differences between the effect of governance and ownership characteristics of family and non-family firms is averaged out when running the models for the full sample (family and non-family firms) as could be seen in Table 8.3.

We conducted additional tests to rule out the possibility that the above results are not robust. First, we tested the sensitivity of our results to the presence of non-linear effects, adding in model (8.2) the squared family ownership ($fown^2$). Table 8.4 reports the results; they suggest the possible presence of non-linear effects, stronger in the case of non-family firms, but the inflationary effects on estimated coefficients and standard errors of introducing the squared ownership has to be taken into account.

**Table 8.4** Robustness check: 2SLS results with non-linear effects

| | All firms | | Non-family firms | | Family firms | |
|---|---|---|---|---|---|---|
| | Model (8.2) | | Model (8.2) | | Model (8.2) | |
| | Coeff | Std err | Coeff | Std err | Coeff | Std err |
| Intercept | 2.166 | 0.050*** | 2.104 | 0.062*** | 2.394 | 0.108*** |
| bsize | 0.002 | 0.001 | 0.002 | 0.002 | 0.000 | 0.003 |
| fboard | 0.063 | 0.050 | 0.849 | 0.180*** | 0.080 | 0.054 |
| fown | −0.232 | 0.053*** | −4.689 | 0.766*** | −0.591 | 0.223*** |
| $fown^2$ | 0.392 | 0.079*** | 22.442 | 4.717*** | 0.639 | 0.212*** |
| bgd | 0.102 | 0.035*** | 0.147 | 0.047*** | 0.017 | 0.058 |
| bcd | 0.034 | 0.018* | 0.077 | 0.022*** | −0.062 | 0.036* |
| size | −0.084 | 0.003*** | −0.086 | 0.004*** | −0.077 | 0.006*** |
| envses | 0.033 | 0.010*** | 0.043 | 0.012*** | 0.013 | 0.016 |
| roa | 0.269 | 0.078*** | 0.37 | 0.105*** | −0.131 | 0.145 |
| r&s | −0.276 | 0.111** | −0.265 | 0.144* | 0.045 | 0.223 |
| Industry | Yes | | Yes | | Yes | |
| Country | Yes | | Yes | | Yes | |
| Years | Yes | | Yes | | Yes | |
| Adj. $R^2$ | 0.282 | | 0.283 | | 0.333 | |

Note. This table presents two least squares (2SLS) results based on our model (8.2). The sample contains 3820 firm-year observations (2513 non-family and 1307 family firm obs) for the period 2013–2022. The dependent variable is the ESG controversies score, the independent variables are board gender diversity (bgd), board size (bsize), board cultural diversity (bcd), family ownership (fown) and squared ownership ($fown^2$), family members on board (fboard), firm dimension (size), profitability (roa), environmental sensitivity (envses), research and development expenditure (r&d), and Industry, Country and Year dummies. Significance: *p<.10 level, **p<.05 level, ***p<.01 level

**Table 8.5** Robustness check: 2SLS results with alternative definitions of family firm

| | Non-family firms | | | | Family firms | | | |
|---|---|---|---|---|---|---|---|---|
| | F-firms when fown>10% | | F-firms when fown>15% | | F-firms when fown>10% | | F-firms when fown>15% | |
| | Coeff | Std err | Coeff | Std err | Coeff | Std err | Coeff | Std err |
| Intercept | 2.029 | 0.062*** | 2.216 | 0.075*** | 2.325 | 0.092*** | 2.227 | 0.093*** |
| bsize | 0.001 | 0.002 | 0.001 | 0.002 | 0.001 | 0.002 | −0.002 | 0.002 |
| fboard | −0.288 | 0.423 | 0.314 | 0.305 | 0.075 | 0.054 | 0.097 | 0.054* |
| fown | −1.014 | 0.664 | −1.375 | 0.289*** | 0.117 | 0.038*** | 0.065 | 0.040 |
| bgd | 0.147 | 0.047*** | 0.166 | 0.047*** | 0.035 | 0.058 | 0.026 | 0.059 |
| bcd | 0.097 | 0.022*** | 0.092 | 0.022*** | −0.101 | 0.036*** | −0.125 | 0.036*** |
| size | −0.08 | 0.004*** | −0.083 | 0.004*** | −0.085 | 0.006*** | −0.074 | 0.006 |
| envses | 0.037 | 0.012*** | 0.053 | 0.013*** | 0.026 | 0.016 | 0.007 | 0.017 |
| roa | 0.337 | 0.104*** | 0.348 | 0.104*** | −0.119 | 0.149 | −0.142 | 0.148 |
| r&s | −0.219 | 0.143 | −0.188 | 0.144 | −0.238 | 0.231 | −0.208 | 0.229 |
| Industry | Yes | | Yes | | Yes | | Yes | |
| Country | Yes | | Yes | | Yes | | Yes | |
| Years | Yes | | Yes | | Yes | | Yes | |
| R-squared | 0.261 | | 0.279 | | 0.342 | | 0.322 | |

Note. This table presents two least squares (2SLS) results based on our model (8.2). The sample contains 3820 firm-year observations (2513 non-family and 1307 family firm obs) for the period 2013–2022. The dependent variable is the ESG controversies score, the independent variables are board gender diversity (bgd), board size (bsize), board cultural diversity (bcd), family ownership (fown), family members on board (fboard), firm dimension (size), profitability (roa), environmental sensitivity (envses), research and development expenditure (r&d), and Industry, Country and Year dummies. Significance: *p<.10 level, **p<.05 level, ***p<.01 level

Second, we explored the possibility that our results were influenced by the definition of family firm, using alternatives ownership thresholds (10% and 15% of voting shares) for family firm identification. Table 8.5 presents the results for these alternative family firm definitions. We note that the main findings are robust to different definitions of family firms, the results for the effect of family ownership and board cultural and gender diversity on the likelihood of incurring in ESG controversies are consistent with the baseline analysis presented in Table 8.3.

Third, we explored the possibility of the existence of possible interaction effects between family ownership and board characteristics, introducing in model (8.2) an interaction effect between family ownership and board cultural diversity (fown x bcd). Results, shown in Table 8.6, indicate that the interaction effect (fown x bcd) is significant for both family and non-family businesses but with opposite sign, confirming the different impact that these governance variables have on the likelihood of incurring in ESG controversies for family and non-family firms.

We conclude that our baseline analysis in Table 8.3, and the robustness tests presented in the following three tables, provide overall support for the hypothesis that in family firms, in comparison with non-family firms, greater ownership concentration reduces the likelihood of incurring in ESG controversies (Hypothesis

**Table 8.6** Robustness check: 2SLS results with family ownership and cultural diversity interaction effect

| | All firms | | Non-family firms | | Family firms | |
|---|---|---|---|---|---|---|
| | Model (8.2) with interaction | | Model (8.2) with interaction | | Model (8.2) with interaction | |
| | Coeff | Std err | Coeff | Std err | Coeff | Std err |
| Intercept | 2.125 | 0.051*** | 2.023 | 0.061*** | 2.303 | 0.098*** |
| bsize | 0.001 | 0.001 | 0.000 | 0.002 | −0.001 | 0.002 |
| fboard | 0.022 | 0.049 | 0.275 | 0.182 | 0.067 | 0.054 |
| fown | 0.068 | 0.025*** | 0.748 | 0.260*** | −0.019 | 0.059 |
| bgd | 0.098 | 0.035*** | 0.142 | 0.046*** | 0.05 | 0.057 |
| bcd | 0.061 | 0.021*** | 0.098 | 0.022*** | −0.267 | 0.095*** |
| size | −0.081 | 0.003*** | −0.079 | 0.004*** | −0.079 | 0.006*** |
| envses | 0.035 | 0.010*** | 0.046 | 0.012*** | 0.007 | 0.016 |
| roa | 0.234 | 0.078*** | 0.323 | 0.103*** | −0.155 | 0.145 |
| r&s | −0.290 | 0.112*** | −0.247 | 0.142* | 0.047 | 0.224 |
| fown x bcd | −0.300 | 0.081*** | −5.552 | 0.591*** | 0.549 | 0.233** |
| Industry | Yes | | Yes | | Yes | |
| Country | Yes | | Yes | | Yes | |
| Years | Yes | | Yes | | Yes | |
| R-squared | 0.281 | | 0.303 | | 0.329 | |

Note. This table presents two least squares (2SLS) results based on our models (8.1) and (8.2). The sample contains 3820 firm-year observations (2513 non-family and 1307 family firm obs) for the period 2013–2022. The dependent variable is the ESG controversies score, the independent variables are board gender diversity (bgd), board size (bsize), board cultural diversity (bcd), family ownership (fown) and squared ownership ($fown^2$), family members on board (fboard), firm dimension (size), profitability (roa), environmental sensitivity (envses), research and development expenditure (r&d), and Industry, Country, and Year dummies. Significance: *p<.10 level, **p<.05 level, ***p<.01 level

H1). On the contrary, greater board cultural diversity in family firms has a negative effect and is associated with higher ESG performance failures (Hypothesis H2).

## 8.5 Theoretical, Managerial, and Regulatory Implications and Limitations

The results of this study have several important implications at the theoretical, managerial, and regulatory levels, which warrant further investigation to better understand the dynamics that shape firms' exposure to ESG controversies, particularly in family businesses. In particular, the findings carry important implications for firms, regulators, and investors committed to promoting sustainable business practices.

These findings have implications for firms regarding risk exposure, as they indicate that board characteristics can enhance firms' ESG commitment and mitigate ESG controversies that are detrimental to financial performance and reputation

(Nirino et al., 2021). A board that promotes comprehensive and transparent ESG disclosure signals its commitment to carefully managing non-financial risks. This, in turn, reduces shareholder and stakeholder exposure to reputational and regulatory uncertainty.

The study contributes to the theoretical debate on the relationship between ownership structure, governance, and sustainability, extending the application of the Socioemotional Wealth perspective (Gómez-Mejía et al., 2007) and Legitimacy Theory (Suchman, 1995) in the context of ESG controversies. The results reinforce the idea that family businesses, especially when they maintain active control, tend to favor behaviors consistent with reputation protection, generational continuity, and social legitimacy, thereby reducing the propensity to engage in ESG controversies (Berrone et al., 2012; Gavana et al., 2017). However, the adverse effect of board cultural diversity on the boards of family firms highlights the need for a more articulated theoretical reflection on the trade-offs between institutional openness and internal cohesion. This suggests that while diversity can enhance the board's informational and relational capital, it may also lead to value misalignment and decision-making frictions when not supported by inclusive leadership and structured governance processes, especially in informally governed family firms (Ponomareva et al., 2022; DasGupta, 2025). The theoretical contribution, therefore, lies in understanding the contingent conditions under which diversity is an advantage or a vulnerability in ESG risk management.

For family businesses, the results indicate that maintaining strong family ownership control can be a strategic asset in preventing ESG controversies, owing to a reputation-oriented approach and a long-term vision (Gómez-Mejía et al., 2011). However, such benefits are more likely when a formal governance structure, transparent practices, and an active ESG orientation accompany strong family control. Diversity management on boards requires proactive approaches, as the inclusion of culturally diverse members can only be beneficial if accompanied by structured decision-making processes, inclusive leadership, and internal mediation skills (Cacciotti & Ucbasaran, 2018; Paolone et al., 2024). The adoption of ESG-sensitive board member selection and training practices can strengthen a company's reputational resilience and prevent conflicts. Finally, companies should consider board size as a critical variable in ESG management, as while larger boards can foster greater diversity of skills and perspectives, in family businesses, they can increase management complexity and hinder timely decision-making (Che & Langli, 2015).

For stakeholders, particularly investors, customers, and local communities, the results suggest that strong family control on the company can serve as an indicator of its ESG responsibility. It enhances the credibility of signals indicating a genuine commitment to ESG disclosure, beyond formal compliance, thereby reducing the likelihood of ESG controversies. Institutional investors should analyze not only the ownership structure but also the degree of family influence and the characteristics of the board. These results are relevant for investors seeking to identify the key sources of information necessary to assess ESG risks and, more generally, a firm's risk management policies (Solomon & Solomon, 2006). These elements can strengthen stakeholder trust and serve as key criteria in responsible investment decisions. In particular, these results are of interest to environmental and socially responsible investors, as they highlight governance characteristics that may signal a proactive approach by the company to comply with ESG regulations and reduce the likelihood of controversies and the severity of their outcomes.

From the regulators' perspective, the importance of promoting governance tools to enhance the effectiveness of board diversity is evident. Our evidence supports the implementation of targeted governance policies that ensure board diversity becomes a functional element of decision-making, particularly in the context of family-led organizations. The findings highlight the need to adopt measures that facilitate the effective inclusion of diverse perspectives, ensuring they are not merely a form of regulatory compliance but can also be positively integrated into boards characterized by a family culture. In this respect, guidelines tailored to family firms could focus on ESG-specific training for top management, the disclosure of sustainability practices, and the strategic integration of environmental and social goals, serving as a lever for reducing systemic ESG risk (Jucá et al., 2024; Samsudin et al., 2025).

While providing significant evidence on the link between governance, ownership structure, and ESG controversies, this study has some limitations that open areas for further exploration. In particular, the quantitative analysis, however robust, does not fully capture the organizational and cultural logic that may explain why specific board configurations, such as cultural diversity, increase ESG risk in family businesses. The use of secondary data does not allow us to investigate how diversity is perceived, managed, or integrated into decision-making processes, nor whether it generates tension or dysfunctional dynamics within family boards. Qualitative studies based on interviews with board members, managers, and family members could offer valuable insights into these dynamics, revealing informal mechanisms, relationships of trust, value conflicts, or exclusionary practices that are not detectable in quantitative studies. Furthermore, a qualitative approach would enable us to assess the extent to which family culture, leadership, and business history influence boards' actual ability to act as guardians of ESG risk prevention.

Our primary proxy for controversies is sourced from Refinitiv Eikon, and, where possible, we have compared our measure with available alternative ESG controversy indicators for a subsample of firms, finding a high degree of consistency. Limited coverage prevents us from entirely replacing or duplicating the measure to rerun the analyses using alternative ESG controversy scores, and we acknowledge this as a data limitation and a future research avenue.

Finally, the sample is tilted toward larger and more visible firms (particularly in France and Germany), which are more likely to be covered by ESG databases and to disclose detailed governance information. We acknowledge this limitation and emphasize that our findings are most representative of large, listed European firms rather than smaller or unlisted family businesses. Focusing on listed European non-financial firms limits generalizability to other geographical or institutional contexts, such as those outside Europe, emerging markets, or unlisted companies, where the dynamics among family, governance, and sustainability may follow substantially different logics.

The ideas for future research emerging from our empirical analysis will be discussed in the last chapter, where the agenda for future studies will be presented.

## References

Ab Aziz, N. H., Alshdaifat, S. M., & Al Amosh, H. (2025). ESG controversies and firm performance in ASEAN: Do board gender diversity and sustainability committee matter? *Business Strategy & Development, 8*(1), e70094.

Alda, M. (2025). The reaction to CSR controversies by institutional investors. *BRQ Business Research Quarterly, 28*(1), 15–36.

Anand, A., Wieszt, A., & Vajda, É. (2025). Decoding the dark sides of family business: A synthesis, and future research agenda. *Review of Managerial Science*, 1–44.

Berrone, P., Cruz, C., & Gomez-Mejia, L. R. (2012). Socioemotional wealth in family firms: Theoretical dimensions, assessment approaches, and agenda for future research. *Family Business Review, 25*(3), 258–279.

Berrone, P., Cruz, C., Gomez-Mejia, L. R., & Larraza-Kintana, M. (2010). Socioemotional wealth and corporate responses to institutional pressures: Do family-controlled firms pollute less? *Administrative Science Quarterly, 55*(1), 82–113.

Boulton, T. J. (2024). Mandatory ESG disclosure, information asymmetry, and litigation risk: Evidence from initial public offerings. *European Financial Management, 30*(5), 2790–2839.

Branco, M. C., & Rodrigues, L. L. (2008). Factors influencing social responsibility disclosure by Portuguese companies. *Journal of Business Ethics, 83*(4), 685–701.

Cacciotti, G., & Ucbasaran, D. (2018). Commentary: Blockholder structures and power mechanisms in family firms. *Entrepreneurship Theory and Practice, 42*(2), 252–258.

Che, L., & Langli, J. C. (2015). Governance structure and firm performance in private family firms. *Journal of Business Finance & Accounting, 42*(9–10), 1216–1250.

Cheung, K. Y., & Lai, C. Y. (2023). The impacts of business ethics and diversity on ESG disclosure: Evidence from Hong Kong. *Journal of Corporate Accounting & Finance, 34*(4), 208–221.

Chou, S. Y., Chang, T., & Han, B. (2016). A Buddhist application of corporate social responsibility: Qualitative evidence from a case study of a small Thai family business. *Small Enterprise Research, 23*(2), 116–134.

Chrisman, J. J., Chua, J. H., & Sharma, P. (2005). Trends and directions in the development of a strategic management theory of the family firm. *Entrepreneurship Theory and Practice, 29*(5), 555–575.

Coles, J. L., Daniel, N. D., & Naveen, L. (2008). Boards: Does one size fit all? *Journal of Financial Economics, 87*(2), 329–356.

Cruz, C., Justo, R., Larraza-Kintana, M., & Garces-Galdeano, L. (2019). When do women make a better table? Examining the influence of women directors on family firm's corporate social performance. *Entrepreneurship Theory and Practice, 43*(2), 282–301.

da Costa, M. M., de Almeida Bizarria, F. P., Ribeiro, R. M., & Mesquita, M. D. S. S. (2023). Determinants of board size: A longitudinal analysis with 194 firms listed on the B3 S/A. *International Journal of Economics and Finance, 15*(4), 1–60.

Dal Maso, L., Basco, R., Bassetti, T., & Lattanzi, N. (2020). Family ownership and environmental performance: The mediation effect of human resource practices. *Business Strategy and the Environment, 29*(3), 1548–1562.

DasGupta, R. (2025). National culture and environmental, social, governance controversies: A cross-country evidence. *Applied Economics, 57*(26), 3642–3659.

Deegan, C. (2002). Introduction: The legitimising effect of social and environmental disclosures–a theoretical foundation. *Accounting, Auditing & Accountability Journal, 15*(3), 282–311.

Diéguez-Soto, J., Campos-Valenzuela, M., Callejón-Gil, Á. M., & Aldeanueva-Fernández, I. (2024). Family firm heterogeneity on CSR approach: A socioemotional(SEW) perspective. *BRQ Business Research Quarterly, 27*(4), 443–466.

Dowling, J., & Pfeffer, J. (1975). Organizational legitimacy: Social values and organizational behavior. *Pacific Sociological Review, 18*(1), 122–136.

Dsouza, S., Krishnamoorthy, K., Kayani, U., Nawaz, F., & Hasan, F. (2025). Sustainable investing: ESG effectiveness and market value in OECD regions. *Cogent Economics & Finance, 13*(1), 2445147.

Duong, T. Q., & Huang, Y. C. (2025). Extending the impact of ESG on firm performance: The moderation effects of ESG controversies and R&D investment. *International Journal of Innovation and Sustainable Development, 19*(2), 224–241.

Dutt, M., Jain, R., Sharma, D., & Bhattacharya, S. (2025). Corporate financial performance in the wake of ESG controversies: The Indian firm context. *Australasian Accounting, Business and Finance Journal, 19*(1).

Elamer, A. A., & Boulhaga, M. (2024). ESG controversies and corporate performance: The moderating effect of governance mechanisms and ESG practices. *Corporate Social Responsibility and Environmental Management, 31*(4), 3312–3327.

Fathoni, A. F., Hanafi, M. M., & Tandelilin, E. (2025). The effects of ESG controversies and women on boards on ESG-washing behavior: Global evidence from the banking industry. *Banks and Bank Systems, 20*(2), 1.

Gallego-Álvarez, I., & Pucheta-Martínez, M. C. (2022a). Board competences and CSR reporting: The moderating role of CEO power: Las competencias del consejo de administración y los informes de RSC: el papel moderador del poder del CEO. *Revista de Contabilidad-Spanish Accounting Review, 25*(2), 282–301.

Gallego-Álvarez, I., & Pucheta-Martínez, M. C. (2022b). Sustainable development through the effect of board diversity and CEO duality on corporate risk: Does the state-owned enterprises matter? *Sustainable Development, 30*(6), 1462–1476.

Gavana, G., Gottardo, P., & Moisello, A. M. (2017). Sustainability reporting in family firms: A panel data analysis. *Sustainability, 9*(1), 38.

Gidage, M., & Bhide, S. (2025). Impact of ESG performance on financial risk in energy firms: Evidence from developing countries. *International Journal of Energy Sector Management, 19*(4), 913–939.

Gomez-Mejia, L. R., Cruz, C., Berrone, P., & De Castro, J. (2011). The bind that ties: Socioemotional wealth preservation in family firms. *Academy of Management Annals, 5*(1), 653–707.

Gómez-Mejía, L. R., Haynes, K. T., Núñez-Nickel, M., Jacobson, K. J., & Moyano-Fuentes, J. (2007). Socioemotional wealth and business risks in family-controlled firms: Evidence from Spanish olive oil mills. *Administrative Science Quarterly, 52*(1), 106–137.

González, M., Guzmán, A., Pombo, C., & Trujillo, M. A. (2013). Family firms and debt: Risk aversion versus risk of losing control. *Journal of Business Research, 66*(11), 2308–2320.

Greco, G., Ferramosca, S., & Allegrini, M. (2014). Exploring intellectual capital in family firms. An empirical investigation. *International Journal of Learning and Intellectual Capital, 11*(2), 91–106.

Gupta, P., & Chauhan, S. (2023). Dynamics of corporate governance mechanisms-family firms' performance relationship-a meta-analytic review. *Journal of Business Research, 154*, 113299.

Hughes, M., Hu, Q., Simeonova, B., Ge, B., Issah, W. B., Jack, S., & Dai, S. (2025). ESG in family firms: A review of research, regulations and practice guidance.

Juca, M. N., Muren, P. D., Valentinčič, A., & Ichev, R. (2024). The impact of ESG controversies on the financial performance of firms: An analysis of industry and country clusters. *Borsa Istanbul Review, 24*(6), 1305–1315.

Katmon, N., Mohamad, Z. Z., Norwani, N. M., & Farooque, O. A. (2019). Comprehensive board diversity and quality of corporate social responsibility disclosure: Evidence from an emerging market. *Journal of Business Ethics, 157*(2), 447–481.

Khan, I., Khan, I., & Saeed, B. B. (2019). Does board diversity affect quality of corporate social responsibility disclosure? Evidence from Pakistan. *Corporate Social Responsibility and Environmental Management, 26*(6), 1371–1381.

Kim, E. H., & Lyon, T. P. (2015). Greenwash vs. brownwash: Exaggeration and undue modesty in corporate sustainability disclosure. *Organization Science, 26*(3), 705–723.

Kim, H. J., Ahn, T. W., & Yi, J. (2025). ESG controversies and firm value: Moderating role of ESG performance. *Asia-Pacific Journal of Financial Studies, 54*(2), 228–269.

Le Breton-Miller, I., Miller, D., & Lester, R. H. (2011). Stewardship or agency? A social embeddedness reconciliation of conduct and performance in public family businesses. *Organization Science, 22*(3), 704–721.

Li, J., Zhao, F., Chen, S., Jiang, W., Liu, T., & Shi, S. (2017). Gender diversity on boards and firms' environmental policy. *Business Strategy and the Environment, 26*(3), 306–315.

Liu, B., & Zhang, X. (2024). The impact of ESG and executive structure on the default risk of family businesses: Evidence from China. *Finance Research Letters, 61*, 104956.

López-González, E., Martínez-Ferrero, J., & García-Meca, E. (2019). Corporate social responsibility in family firms: A contingency approach. *Journal of Cleaner Production, 211*, 1044–1064.

Miller, D., Le Breton-Miller, I., & Lester, R. H. (2011). Family and lone founder ownership and strategic behaviour: Social context, identity, and institutional logics. *Journal of Management Studies, 48*(1), 1–25.

Muhammad, H., & Farooq, M. (2025). The effectiveness of board gender diversity and sustainability committees in mitigating ESG controversies. *Meditari Accountancy Research.* https://doi.org/10.1108/medar-07-2024-2565

Muttakin, M. B., Khan, A., & Subramaniam, N. (2015). Firm characteristics, board diversity and corporate social responsibility: Evidence from Bangladesh. *Pacific Accounting Review, 27*(3), 353–372.

Naciti, V. (2019). Corporate governance and board of directors: The effect of a board composition on firm sustainability performance. *Journal of Cleaner Production, 237*, 117727.

Nadeem, M., Gyapong, E., & Ahmed, A. (2020). Board gender diversity and environmental, social, and economic value creation: Does family ownership matter? *Business Strategy and the Environment, 29*(3), 1268–1284.

Ng, P. Y., & Hamilton, R. T. (2024). Socioemotional wealth and the innovativeness of family SMEs in the United Arab Emirates. *Journal of Small Business & Entrepreneurship, 36*(1), 158–181.

Nimer, K., Abughazaleh, N., Tahat, Y., & Hossain, M. (2025). Family business, ESG, and firm age in the GCC corporations: Building on the socioemotional wealth (SEW) model. *Journal of Risk and Financial Management, 18*(5), 241.

Nirino, N., Santoro, G., Miglietta, N., & Quaglia, R. (2021). Corporate controversies and company's financial performance: Exploring the moderating role of ESG practices. *Technological Forecasting and Social Change, 162*, 120341.

Paolone, F., Pozzoli, M., Chhabra, M., & Di Vaio, A. (2024). Cultural and gender diversity for ESG performance towards knowledge sharing: Empirical evidence from European banks. *Journal of Knowledge Management, 28*(11), 106–131.

Ponomareva, Y., Federo, R., Aguilera, R. V., & Collin, S. O. (2022). The cost of conformity to good governance: Board design and compensation. *Corporate Governance: An International Review, 30*(4), 399–420.

Post, C., & Byron, K. (2015). Women on boards and firm financial performance: A meta-analysis. *Academy of Management Journal, 58*(5), 1546–1571.

Padungsaksawasdi, C., & Treepongkaruna, S. (2024). Corporate social responsibility, board characteristics, and family business in Thailand. *Corporate Social Responsibility and Environmental Management, 31*(2), 1340–1353.

Rodríguez-Ariza, L., Cuadrado-Ballesteros, B., Martínez-Ferrero, J., & García-Sánchez, I. M. (2017). The role of female directors in promoting CSR practices: An international comparison between family and non-family businesses. *Business Ethics: A European Review, 26*(2), 162–174.

Samsudin, Z. A., Sahu, M., Alahdal, W. M., Abd Majid, N., & Muhmad, S. N. (2025). The moderating effect of ESG controversies on the relationship between CSR committee and ESG performance: Malaysian evidence. *Business Strategy & Development, 8*(3), e70158.

Sari, M., Joni, J., & Ginting, E. K. S. B. (2024). How does family business affect the association between corporate social responsibility disclosure and cost of debt in Indonesia? *Business Strategy & Development, 7*(3), e395.

Sassen, R., Hinze, A. K., & Hardeck, I. (2016). Impact of ESG factors on firm risk in Europe. *Journal of Business Economics, 86*(8), 867–904.

Seckin-Halac, D., Erdener-Acar, E., & Zengin-Karaibrahimoglu, Y. (2021). Ownership and corporate social responsibility: "The power of the female touch". *European Management Journal, 39*(6), 695–709.

Shakri, I. H., Chung, C. Y., & Ryu, D. (2025). Do board networks fuel ESG controversies? *Finance Research Letters*, 107641.

Sial, M. S., Chunmei, Z., & Khuong, N. V. (2019). Do female and independent directors explain the two-way relationship between corporate social responsibility and earnings management of Chinese listed firms? *International Journal of Accounting & Information Management, 27*(3), 442–460.

Solomon, J. F., & Solomon, A. (2006). Private social, ethical and environmental disclosure. *Accounting, Auditing & Accountability Journal, 19*(4), 564–591.

Song, L., He, W., Zou, L., & Xu, M. (2025). Do female family directors affect corporate social responsibility in Chinese family firms? *Asia Pacific Business Review, 31*(2), 280–300.

Suchman, M. C. (1995). Managing legitimacy: Strategic and institutional approaches. *Academy of Management Review, 20*(3), 571–610.

Tan, X., & Tuluca, S. A. (2024). Liquidity and profitability's effect on the environmental, social, and governance scores of S&P 500 companies. *Corporate Governance and Sustainability Review, 8*(4), 22–29.

Treepongkaruna, S., Kyaw, K., & Jiraporn, P. (2024). ESG controversies and corporate governance: Evidence from board size. *Business Strategy and the Environment, 33*(5), 4218–4232.

Villalonga, B., & Amit, R. (2010). Family control of firms and industries. *Financial Management, 39*(3), 863–904.

Wang, H., & Wang, W. (2024). Chairperson gender, policy compliance and ESG performance of family firms. *International Review of Economics & Finance, 96*, 103714.

Wang, Y. C., Tsai, J. J., & Lin, H. W. W. (2013). The influence of board structure on firm performance. *Journal of Global Business Management, 9*(2), 7.

Yilmaz, M. K., Hacioglu, U., Tatoglu, E., Aksoy, M., & Duran, S. (2023). Measuring the impact of board gender and cultural diversity on corporate governance and social performance: Evidence from emerging markets. *Economic Research-Ekonomska istraživanja, 36*(2).

Zaid, M. A., Wang, M., Adib, M., Sahyouni, A., & Abuhijleh, S. T. (2020). Boardroom nationality and gender diversity: Implications for corporate sustainability performance. *Journal of Cleaner Production, 251*, 119652.

Zavyalova, A., Pfarrer, M. D., Reger, R. K., & Shapiro, D. L. (2012). Managing the message: The effects of firm actions and industry spillovers on media coverage following wrongdoing. *Academy of Management Journal, 55*(5), 1079–1101.

# Chapter 9
# Other Types of Risks in Family Firms

**Abstract** This chapter analyzes the response of family businesses to systemic crises, such as the COVID-19 pandemic and the 2008 global financial crisis (Exogenous crises and pandemic resilience-orange/blue cluster), highlighting the ambivalence between resilience and vulnerability. The emergence of a predominantly reactive resilience, based on internal cohesion, relational capital, and financial prudence, has enabled family businesses to mitigate short-term impacts; however, it has also highlighted limitations in their transformative capacity and in their structured risk management. The lack of formal Enterprise Risk Management systems and the overlap between family and decision-making logics have reduced organizational adaptability. However, experiences of forced innovation, intergenerational leadership, and digital transformations suggest the emergence of evolutionary trajectories toward more anticipatory forms of resilience. This chapter presents a critical, comparative analysis of family behaviors in the context of shocks, highlighting theoretical implications for redefining resilience and offering managerial recommendations to enhance the systemic preparedness of family businesses.

**Keywords** Exogenous shocks · COVID-19 · Financial crisis · Resilience · Risk

## 9.1 Pandemic and Family Resilience: Emerging Strategies in Response to COVID-19

During the COVID-19 pandemic, family businesses have faced profound discontinuity, redefining the relationship between risk and business continuity (Kraus et al., 2020). Recent literature highlights a significant evolution in decision-making practices that has at times challenged the firms' original risk aversion. Leppäaho and Ritala (2022), for example, illustrate how a Finnish family business, despite being characterized by traditional prudence, adopted highly innovative strategies to ensure its survival and preserve its socioemotional capital. Similarly, Glowka et al. (2024) report that, in German family SMEs, the pandemic catalyzed digital transformation, temporarily overcoming risk aversion while maintaining strong family control. In



A. M. Moisello, P. Gottardo, *Risk and Sustainability in Family Businesses*, SpringerBriefs in Finance, https://doi.org/10.1007/978-3-032-19995-9_9

other contexts, responses have been more conservative: Espinosa-Méndez et al. (2023) highlight how many European companies have adopted prudent capital management practices, while Jebran and Chen (2023) observe that, in Asia, corporate restructuring has been accompanied by persistent strategic caution. In Iran, Jahanshahi et al. (2023) document an emphasis on sustainability and the protection of relational and reputational capital. In Latin America, Llanos-Contreras et al. (2021) show that the crisis has amplified operational uncertainty but also reinforced the importance of internal cohesion.

The study by Miroshnychenko et al. (2024) provides a global perspective by analyzing 3350 listed companies across 33 countries and finds that family businesses with strong ownership involvement in management outperformed their non-family counterparts during the pandemic.

From a comparative perspective, Memili & Koç (2023) find that a strong socio-emotional identity has facilitated reputational risk management. Still, the absence of structured risk management systems has been a significant limitation. In Portugal, Santos et al. (2022) report that the adoption of frugal innovation practices has reduced operational risk at the expense of resource sustainability. The Indonesian case, analyzed by Perwitasari et al. (2022), highlights how the overlap between family and business has slowed down strategic responses. Finally, longitudinal studies (Villagrasa et al., 2025) show that the resilience of family businesses has often been reactive rather than anticipatory, based on traditional values and relational resources (Zainal, 2022).

Patel (2025), studying the US context, finds that family businesses have not shown greater resilience than non-family businesses in terms of market performance or volatility. This result, explained by isomorphic institutional pressures, raises doubts about the universality of family resilience, suggesting that in highly liberalized, short-term-oriented contexts, such as the US, the peculiarities of family businesses may constitute a competitive disadvantage rather than an advantage.

Furthermore, the study by Cano-Rubio et al. (2024) highlights the importance of relational and symbolic resilience during the pandemic crisis, emphasizing how family businesses reacted by preserving internal ties and reputational capital, often foregoing drastic restructuring measures. This emphasis on stability and trust fostered a slower but more cohesive response, confirming a more relational approach to risk management than a technical one.

Finally, Jaufenthaler (2023) offers a theoretical reflection on the need to reformulate traditional concepts of family resilience in light of extreme events, suggesting greater integration between reactive resilience, grounded in values and cohesion, and proactive resilience, grounded in structured management tools.

## 9.2 Financial Crisis and Family Businesses

The global financial crisis of 2008 was a crucial test of the resilience of family businesses, providing a unique context for analyzing their behavior in the face of systemic economic and financial shocks (Amann & Jaussaud, 2014). Numerous studies have demonstrated that family involvement in corporate governance significantly affects risk management in highly turbulent contexts. Arrondo-García et al. (2016), analyzing Spanish family businesses, indicate that the presence of a family CEO acts as a stabilizing factor, promoting consistent strategic choices and contributing to relatively more robust performance than in non-family businesses. This decision-making stability was fostered by long-term orientation and a greater aversion to loss of control, both of which encouraged prudent yet resilient behavior.

From a longitudinal perspective, Alharasis et al. (2023) observe that the crisis has led to a profound rethinking of governance within family businesses, prompting them to reconsider their decision-making structures without, however, renouncing the centrality of family values. Despite pressure, these companies have shown a lower propensity to adopt aggressive restructuring, instead favoring the preservation of employment and social stability. This behavior suggests a view of risk that extends beyond the financial dimension, encompassing reputational and value considerations. As Gómez and Rodríguez (2024) demonstrate, this experience has left a lasting "memory of risk," influencing how family businesses respond even in more recent contexts, such as the post-pandemic era. This memory manifests as greater readiness to adopt conservative strategies and to strengthen organizational resilience, albeit with some rigidity in adapting to new circumstances.

Another element of resilience that emerged during the crisis was the territorial roots of family businesses. Amato et al. (2023) demonstrate that companies with strong local ties exhibit a significantly lower propensity to downsize, highlighting a stronger social responsibility toward local communities. This identity bond with the territory has strengthened internal cohesion and external reputation, thereby enhancing organizational resilience.

In the Italian context, Stacchini and Degasperi (2015) report that, during the crisis, family businesses were significantly less likely to default on bank loans than their non-family counterparts, mainly due to lower debt levels and more cautious financial management. However, this same caution reduced the ability to seize investment opportunities during the recovery phase, revealing the ambivalence of crisis management: protective in the short term but potentially limiting in the long term.

D'Aurizio et al. (2015) confirm this interpretation, showing that Italian family businesses had more stable access to bank credit than non-family businesses, thanks to lower information asymmetry. The role of "soft information," based on long-term relationships with banks, proved crucial in maintaining regular financial flows, even during a credit crunch. Similarly, Wieczorek-Kosmala et al. (2021), analyzing Polish family businesses in the post-crisis period, emphasize capital preservation and reluctance to adopt formal financial planning tools. While this approach reduced immediate exposure to systemic risk, it left room for operational vulnerabilities, particularly in sectors subject to high volatility or further exogenous shocks.

On the other hand, Bauweraerts and Colot (2013) highlight in the Belgian case that the resilience of family businesses stems from a combination of absorption capacity and renewal. Family businesses have proven capable of maintaining high levels of self-financing and, in some cases, increasing investment even in the face of contracting demand, revealing a strategic orientation that is not necessarily defensive.

Stafford et al. (2013) propose a comprehensive model of resilience for family businesses in response to environmental disasters and sudden crises, comprising three phases: preparation, adaptation, and recovery. This framework also applies effectively to financial crises, highlighting the crucial role of family cohesion, internal trust, and decision-making flexibility. However, the authors warn that this resilience can be compromised by poorly formalized governance, which hinders the timeliness and effectiveness of organizational responses. In this context, Skare and Porada-Rochon (2021) introduce the perspective of financial cycles, demonstrating that family businesses are less vulnerable to macroeconomic and financial shocks than non-family businesses. According to the authors, this greater stability stems from a combination of conservative strategies, cohesive governance, and a longer-term orientation, which strengthens the capacity to absorb shocks in both the expansionary and recessionary phases of the cycle.

Consistently, Zhou et al. (2017) analyze US family businesses in the S&P 500 and show that those still led by their founders performed better during the crisis, thanks to a lower propensity to overinvest and easier access to credit. The combined effect of strategic prudence and the founder's reputation produced stronger performance than that of their non-family counterparts.

From an integrated European perspective, Riepl et al. (2024) introduce the concept of systemic vulnerability, including not only financial factors but also institutional and reputational elements in risk assessment. The lack of a holistic, structured approach to risk management exposes family businesses to amplified effects during complex, multidimensional crises, such as pandemics or geopolitical instability. Ultimately, the contributions analyzed converge in their view that the 2008 crisis was a transformative event for family businesses, revealing both their strengths—such as financial prudence and internal cohesion—and their structural weaknesses, such as resistance to change and the absence of advanced risk management systems.

## 9.3 Systemic Crises and Family Businesses: Critical Reflections

An examination of the reactions of family businesses to the 2008 financial crisis and the COVID-19 pandemic allows us to identify, in a comparative manner, a series of recurring trajectories in systemic risk management. Although the two crises differ in nature and dynamics, they have highlighted both the distinctive resources of these businesses and their structural fragilities. On the one hand, it is possible to recognize a resilient capacity associated with stable family leadership, internal cohesion, and a long-term value orientation. On the other hand, significant limitations arise from decision-making rigidity, the absence of formalized risk management systems, and the difficulty of responding promptly to complex emergency scenarios.

Among the primary strengths, strategic consistency stands out, supported by management continuity and the family's direct involvement in the business's operations (Arrondo-García et al., 2016; Leppäaho & Ritala, 2022). In both crisis contexts, this continuity has fostered greater organizational stability and the ability to maintain performance under pressure. Relational capital, both internal and external, has proven to be a crucial resource, as the trust built among family members, workers, and stakeholders has served as a shock absorber and a source of resilience in the face of uncertainty (Llanos-Contreras et al., 2021; Cano-Rubio et al., 2024). This cohesion has been intertwined with a long-term vision that prioritizes wealth preservation and social responsibility, even at the expense of short-term efficiency (Jahanshahi et al., 2023; Memili & Koç, 2023). For family businesses, this suggests the need to strengthen relational resources as a strategic asset, as well as risk governance.

Another distinctive feature of family businesses that emerged in both crises is their prudence in managing financial resources. Prudent debt management, long-standing relationships with the banking system, and the use of internal resources have enabled many of them to limit their exposure to liquidity and insolvency risks (D'Aurizio et al., 2015; Stacchini & Degasperi, 2015). From a managerial perspective, this reinforces the importance of a culture of liquidity and financial relationship management, especially in contexts with high systemic risk.

However, the overlap between family and managerial logics tends to slow decision-making, generating organizational rigidity, particularly in the face of sudden shocks that require rapid, flexible responses (Perwitasari et al., 2022; Stafford et al., 2013). In the absence of a structured governance model, the impact of family emotions can interfere with the efficiency of responses. Furthermore, strong risk aversion, although protective in the acute phase, can be a limitation in the recovery phase, where failure to take strategic risks leads to missed opportunities for innovation and growth (Wieczorek-Kosmala et al., 2021; Stacchini & Degasperi, 2015). Family businesses, especially small and medium-sized ones, should invest in structured and preventive tools, including scenario analysis and risk simulation, to make more effective and timely decisions (Verbano & Venturini, 2013).

Shortcomings in the structuring of Enterprise Risk Management systems are another critical issue. In many cases, the absence of an integrated and formal approach to risk management has left family businesses exposed to cumulative risk effects, particularly in prolonged, multidimensional contexts such as the pandemic (Memili & Koç, 2023; Riepl et al., 2024). Family resilience, often grounded in relational resources and historical memory, has been limited in contexts lacking anticipatory capacity and a culture of structured adaptation (Villagrasa et al., 2025; Zainal, 2022). This implies for researchers the opportunity to investigate how resilience can be developed not only relationally but also structurally and technologically.

A further critical element has emerged in the US context, where family businesses have not shown greater resilience than non-family businesses, either in terms of performance or volatility, due to isomorphic pressures and a short-term institutional context (Patel, 2025). This finding prompts us to reconsider the notion of 'natural' resilience in family businesses, acknowledging their dependence on the institutional context and the extent of internal structuring. For policymakers, it is necessary to differentiate support instruments according to the organizational maturity of family businesses to promote transformative resilience.

The analysis of family businesses' responses to recent systemic crises, notably the COVID-19 pandemic, raises important questions at both theoretical and operational levels. From a conceptual perspective, the empirical evidence gathered enables us to move beyond the traditional interpretation that family businesses are inherently risk-averse. On the contrary, their propensity to take risks appears to be strongly mediated by value-based objectives—such as generational continuity, reputation, and the protection of socioemotional capital—which can trigger even bold entrepreneurial behavior in conditions of extreme discontinuity (Jahanshahi et al., 2023; Leppäaho & Ritala, 2022). This evidence opens new theoretical perspectives on the integration between SEW and risk-taking, suggesting that dichotomous approaches should be overcome and non-linear models of entrepreneurial behavior in critical contexts should be developed.

As several studies have shown, family businesses can adopt innovative, rapid solutions, including the digitalization of processes and the reconfiguration of business models (Glowka et al., 2024). However, such reactions are often temporary, confirming a resilience that is more reactive than anticipatory (Villagrasa et al., 2025).

In this sense, it becomes theoretically relevant to distinguish between adaptive resilience and transformative resilience. The former manifests as the use of pre-existing relational and asset resources to overcome the shock; the latter entails an evolution of decision-making and organizational models, grounded in strategic learning and the formalization of risk governance tools. The lack of structured ERM systems is a cross-cutting vulnerability that limits the transformative capacity of family businesses. At the same time, there is growing interest in the role of second and third generations, who bring visions more oriented toward change, innovation, and formalized risk management (Cano-Rubio et al., 2024), with theoretical implications for the study of the intergenerational evolution of family capabilities.

At the operational level, the managerial implications of these findings are numerous and converge on the need to strengthen the ability of family businesses to manage uncertainty in a structured and systemic manner. A first guideline concerns the transition from a predominantly reactive approach, based on trust networks and emergency responses, to an integrated, preventive view of risk that includes business continuity plans, digital monitoring tools, and scenario simulations. Secondly, the importance of professionalizing governance is confirmed: companies that have integrated external expertise into their boards or adopted formalized decision-making processes have demonstrated greater readiness to respond to crises (Stafford et al., 2013; Riepl et al., 2024). However, a delicate balance remains between rationalization and tradition: while family values are a fundamental source of identity, they can also constrain the adoption of transformative strategies, delaying urgent or unconventional decisions (Perwitasari et al., 2022).

External stakeholders—such as policymakers, financial institutions, and consultants—are also called upon to rethink their approaches to family businesses. Public policies should recognize their structural specificity and promote support tools that enhance their social and reputational resilience, while encouraging the transition to more professional models better equipped to manage multidimensional shocks. Credit institutions, for their part, could strengthen their creditworthiness assessment by incorporating qualitative indicators related to reputation and relational continuity, particularly in contexts characterized by high information asymmetry. Finally, the role of consulting is crucial in promoting tailor-made capacity-building processes that can support entrepreneurial families in structuring risk management systems consistent with their identity, yet also adequate to the challenges of turbulent contexts.

## References


Alharasis, E. E., Alhadab, M., Alidarous, M., Jamaani, F., & Alkhwaldi, A. F. (2023). The impact of COVID-19 on the relationship between auditor industry specialization and audit fees: Empirical evidence from Jordan. *Journal of Financial Reporting and Accounting*. https://doi.org/10.1108/jfra-01-2023-0052

Amann, B., & Jaussaud, J. (2014). Family and non-family business resilience in an economic downturn. In *Japan's 'Lost Decade'* (pp. 69–89). Routledge.

Amato, S., Patuelli, A., Basco, R., & Lattanzi, N. (2023). Family firms amidst the global financial crisis: A territorial embeddedness perspective on downsizing. *Journal of Business Ethics, 183*(1), 213–236.

Arrondo-García, R., Fernández-Méndez, C., & Menéndez-Requejo, S. (2016). The growth and performance of family businesses during the global financial crisis: The role of the generation in control. *Journal of Family Business Strategy, 7*(4), 227–237.

Bauweraerts, J., & Colot, O. (2013). How do family firms deal with the crisis? *International Advances in Economic Research, 19*(3), 313–314.

Cano-Rubio, M., Barroso, A., Sanguino, R., Valentino, A., Calabro, A., & Basco, R. (2024). We don't fire! Family firms and employment change during the COVID-19 pandemic. *Journal of Family Business Management, 14*(6), 1153–1172.

D'Aurizio, L., Oliviero, T., & Romano, L. (2015). Family firms, soft information and bank lending in a financial crisis. *Journal of Corporate Finance, 33*, 279–292.

Espinosa-Méndez, C., Maquieira, C. P., & Arias, J. T. (2023). The impact of ESG performance on the value of family firms: The moderating role of financial constraints and agency problems. *Sustainability, 15*(7), 6176.

Glowka, G., Eller, R., Peters, M., & Zehrer, A. (2024). Risk perception in small-and medium-sized hospitality family enterprises. *Tourism Review*. https://doi.org/10.1108/tr-06-2023-0421

Gómez, J. M., & Rodríguez, Y. E. (2024). Strategic renewal of family firms to face vulnerability risks during times of crisis. *International Journal of Social Economics, 51*(12), 1538–1564.

Jahanshahi, A. A., Mendoza, M. I. R., & Aguilar-Rodríguez, I. E. (2023). Unveiling resilience: Strategic responses, success factors, and challenges faced by Latin American female entrepreneurs amid the COVID-19 pandemic. *IEEE Engineering Management Review, 52*(1), 92–107.
Jaufenthaler, P. (2023). A safe haven in times of crisis: The appeal of family companies as employers amid the COVID-19 pandemic. *Journal of Family Business Strategy, 14*(1), 100520.
Jebran, K., & Chen, S. (2023). Can we learn lessons from the past? COVID-19 crisis and corporate governance responses. *International Journal of Finance & Economics, 28*(1), 421–429.
Kraus, S., Clauss, T., Breier, M., Gast, J., Zardini, A., & Tiberius, V. (2020). The economics of COVID-19: Initial empirical evidence on how family firms in five European countries cope with the corona crisis. *International Journal of Entrepreneurial Behavior & Research, 26*(5), 1067–1092.
Leppäaho, T., & Ritala, P. (2022). Surviving the coronavirus pandemic and beyond: Unlocking family firms' innovation potential across crises. *Journal of Family Business Strategy, 13*(1), 100440.
Llanos-Contreras, O., Arias, J., & Maquieira, C. (2021). Risk taking behavior in Chilean listed family firms: A socioemotional wealth approach. *International Entrepreneurship and Management Journal, 17*(1), 165–184.
Memili, E., & Koç, B. (2023). The antecedents of family firms' resilience to crisis in hospitality and tourism. *International Journal of Hospitality Management, 113*, 103526.
Miroshnychenko, I., Vocalelli, G., De Massis, A., Grassi, S., & Ravazzolo, F. (2024). The COVID-19 pandemic and family business performance. *Small Business Economics, 62*(1), 213–241.
Patel, P. (2025). Rethinking family business resilience: an empirical examination of family firms' performance amid the COVID-19 pandemic in the US. *Applied Economics, 57*(30), 4335–4347.
Perwitasari, D., Setiawan, D., Nurrahmawati, A., & Rahmawati, I. P. (2022). Firm performance during COVID-19 pandemic: Does ownership identity matter? Evidence from Indonesia. *Journal of Risk and Financial Management, 15*(10), 444.
Riepl, J., Mitter, C., & Kuttner, M. (2024). Risk management during the COVID-19 crisis: Insights from an exploratory case study of medium-sized family businesses. *Journal of Management Control, 35*(1), 109–135.
Santos, E., Tavares, V., Tavares, F. O., & Ratten, V. (2022). How is risk different in family and non-family businesses? A comparative statistical analysis during the COVID-19 pandemic. *Journal of Family Business Management, 12*(4), 1113–1130.
Škare, M., & Porada-Rochoń, M. (2021). Measuring the impact of financial cycles on family firms: How to prepare for crisis? *International Entrepreneurship and Management Journal, 17*(3), 1111–1130.
Stacchini, M., & Degasperi, P. (2015). Trust, family businesses and financial intermediation. *Journal of Corporate Finance, 33*, 293–316.
Stafford, K., Danes, S. M., & Haynes, G. W. (2013). Long-term family firm survival and growth considering owning family adaptive capacity and federal disaster assistance receipt. *Journal of Family Business Strategy, 4*(3), 188–200.
Verbano, C., & Venturini, K. (2013). Managing risks in SMEs: A literature review and research agenda. *Journal of Technology Management & Innovation, 8*(3), 186–197.
Villagrasa, J., Escribá-Esteve, A., Donaldson, C., & Sánchez-Peinado, E. (2025). Firms financial strength during crisis periods: Does "familiness" matter? *Journal of Family Business Management, 15*(4), 1087–1111.
Wieczorek-Kosmala, M., Błach, J., & Doś, A. (2021). COVID-19 interruptions and SMEs heterogeneity: Evidence from Poland. *Risks, 9*(9), 161.
Zainal, M. (2022). Innovation orientation and performance of Kuwaiti family businesses: Evidence from the initial period of COVID-19 pandemic. *Journal of Family Business Management, 12*(2), 251–265.
Zhou, H., He, F., & Wang, Y. (2017). Did family firms perform better during the financial crisis? New insights from the S&P 500 firms. *Global Finance Journal, 33*, 88–103.

# Chapter 10
# Conclusions: Contributions to Literature and Lines of Development for Future Research

**Abstract** The concluding chapter presents the study's contributions. Through the integration of bibliometric analysis and conceptual reconstruction, five main areas of contribution emerge: the structured reconstruction of theoretical trajectories; the redefinition of the concept of family resilience; the interpretation of risk as a relational and affective construct; the enhancement of governance as a lever for risk management; and the link between family entrepreneurship, reputation, and sustainability. The chapter concludes with a detailed proposal for future research, structured into five thematic areas related to risk: ownership structures and disclosure; life cycle, succession, and financial structure; innovation and digitalization; internationalization; CSR, ESG, and risk management in terms of reputation and identity.

The aim is to outline a multi-dimensional research agenda capable of capturing the contextual complexity of risk management in family businesses.

**Keywords** Risk framework · Research agenda · Governance · Succession · ESG risk

## 10.1 Contributions to Research on Family Businesses

Bibliometric analysis and in-depth study of the use of theories in research on risk in family businesses offer a structured systematization of a broad but fragmented field of study. They also provide a deeper understanding of the variety of theoretical frameworks used to interpret the relationship between family control, risk, and performance.

Bibliometric analysis enables the visualization and decoding of semantic networks addressing risk in the literature on family businesses, revealing seven main clusters that divide the field into coherent yet interrelated subdomains, ranging from governance and CSR to innovation and succession, and from reputation to pandemic resilience. The most significant finding, however, is the relative marginality of ESG issues. Despite the growing importance of ESG considerations in risk



A. M. Moisello, P. Gottardo, *Risk and Sustainability in Family Businesses*, SpringerBriefs in Finance, https://doi.org/10.1007/978-3-032-19995-9_10

management, they do not emerge as central keywords or as autonomous clusters, indicating a significant research gap in the study of risk in family businesses.

The second contribution, of a theoretical nature, involves identifying the main interpretative lenses that guide impactful studies on family risk: Agency Theory, Behavioral Agency Theory, Socioemotional Wealth Theory, and Stewardship Theory as the dominant frameworks. This theoretical repertoire demonstrates that the family is not merely a structural variable, but a strategic subject that actively engages with the cognitive, affective, and reputational dimensions of risk. While Agency Theory allows us to analyze internal governance conflicts and information opacity (Anderson et al., 2009), behavioral and affective perspectives help explain seemingly conservative decisions such as reluctance to diversify (Gómez-Mejía et al., 2010), a cautious approach to internationalization (George et al., 2005), or a propensity to support CSR for reputational rather than regulatory reasons (Yang et al., 2023). Finally, Stewardship Theory introduces a fiduciary and value-based view of family management, according to which risk is taken not to maximize returns but to protect the firm's symbolic integrity and intergenerational mission (Le Breton-Miller & Miller, 2009; Zellweger & Nason, 2008).

The theoretical and conceptual contributions that emerged from the analyses in Chaps. 2–9 represent a significant advance in understanding risk management within family businesses, particularly in how affective, identity, and generational logics interact with economic and managerial dimensions. The literature review reveals a complex picture characterized by structural ambivalences and contextual conditions that modulate the effectiveness of family businesses in risk management.

A third fundamental contribution concerns the redefinition of the concept of resilience in family businesses. It is not presented as an intrinsic and generalizable quality of the family model, but rather as the outcome of specific organizational processes that combine long-term value orientations with adaptive strategic capabilities. Family businesses demonstrate their capacity to respond positively to crisis scenarios through stable leadership, internal cohesion, and relational trust, both within the family nucleus and in relationships with external stakeholders (Arrondo-García et al., 2016; Leppäaho & Ritala, 2022; Llanos-Contreras et al., 2021). However, this resilience is effective only when accompanied by robust governance structures, an organizational culture open to change, and a concrete capacity to learn from crises (Villagrasa et al., 2024; Memili & Koç, 2023).

A fourth area of contribution concerns the conceptualization of risk as a category that is neither neutral nor unshaped by the family and emotional dynamics that guide decision-making. The approach to risk in family businesses cannot be understood in purely rational or financial terms. It is intrinsically linked to the protection of socioemotional capital, which includes elements such as reputation, generational continuity, and family control (Berrone et al., 2012). These elements influence both risk appetite and risk management, thereby generating strategic behaviors that are consistent with identity values rather than economic optimization criteria. This view significantly broadens classical risk theories by introducing a relational and value-based perspective that explains seemingly conservative decisions, such as the selective adoption of digitalization (Giacomarra et al., 2021; Bornhausen & Wulf, 2024) or the limited use of structured risk management tools (Hiebl et al., 2019), not as symptoms of backwardness, but as an expression of a different rationality, oriented toward safeguarding the internal consistency of the family system.

In line with this approach, a fifth contribution emerges, linked to the reconceptualization of governance's role. The analysis reveals that the characteristics of family governance, in particular, the composition of the board, the inclusion of independent members, and gender and generational diversity, are decisive not only in shaping strategic choices but also in the quality of risk management. Professional, transparent, and pluralistic governance appears to be the enabling condition for transforming emotional resources into stable competitive advantages, while containing the risks associated with information opacity, agency conflicts, and decision-making rigidity (Wu et al., 2020; Roffia et al., 2022). It is not the family nature itself that determines greater or lesser effectiveness in risk management, but rather the ability to build institutional structures that are consistent with family values while remaining open to the market, external control, and learning.

Of particular importance in this context is the link between entrepreneurial orientation and risk management. The analysis indicates that family businesses can demonstrate a high degree of proactivity and a selective propensity for innovation, particularly when there is alignment among generational leadership, strategic vision, and openness to digital transformation (Craig et al., 2014; Zhu & Kang, 2022; Garcia-Piqueres et al., 2019). Entrepreneurial orientation is therefore not a monolithic construct but a dynamic combination of innovativeness, proactivity, and risk-taking that varies with organizational culture, decision-making structures, and the cognitive abilities of the generations in charge. It is precisely this internal heterogeneity—between founders and successors, between identity-based and managerial approaches—that constitutes a fundamental lever in defining the risk management trajectory. Family businesses that successfully combine emotional sensitivity and entrepreneurial pragmatism are better able to respond not only to external crises but also to internal discontinuities, such as succession or market changes (Chalus-Sauvannet et al., 2016).

Ultimately, a significant theoretical insight emerges regarding the role of reputation and corporate social responsibility (CSR) in the development of risk mitigation strategies. Family reputation serves as symbolic capital, reducing the uncertainty perceived by the market, investors, and employees, and constitutes a fundamental resource, especially in weak institutional contexts or opaque markets (Wu et al., 2014; Allison & Anglin, 2025). However, the effectiveness of this capital depends on the consistency between value statements and actual behavior: CSR practices adopted instrumentally or rhetorically risk generating reputational risk (Özbay et al., 2023; Jian et al., 2024). The authentic integration of CSR into decision-making processes, supported by inclusive structures and internal accountability, therefore acts as a lever to strengthen the sustainability, transparency, and resilience of family businesses.

In summary, the contributions presented in these chapters enable a shift away from linear and universalistic approaches to risk management in family businesses toward a relational, contextual, and multidimensional perspective. Family businesses are no longer described as inherently resilient or conservative, but as complex organisms, torn between continuity and change, between emotion and rationality, between identity and the market. It is in this complexity that the added value of the contributions analyzed lies: in offering the literature an interpretive key capable of grasping the structural ambivalences of family governance, its latent strengths, and its implicit risks, within a dynamic logic of adaptation, learning, and transformation.

Finally, the chapter dedicated to ESG controversies in family businesses makes an original contribution to an area that remains largely unexplored in the empirical literature, analyzing the extent to which specific ownership and board characteristics influence the likelihood of such controversies.

The work builds upon studies that apply the construct of Socioemotional Wealth (Gómez-Mejía et al., 2007) and Legitimacy Theory (Suchman, 1995) to interpret the behavior of family businesses regarding sustainability issues. The results confirm that a greater concentration of family ownership, when accompanied by control of the company, is associated with a lower propensity to engage in ESG controversies, suggesting that entrepreneurial families pay greater attention to reputation and value consistency. Conversely, in companies where the family is present only as a residual shareholder but does not hold strategic control, the effect of family ownership can be adverse (Miller et al., 2011).

A further contribution is to show that, in family businesses, cultural diversity on the board is associated with a higher incidence of ESG controversies. Although this result does not allow us to identify the underlying causal mechanisms, it suggests that in family governance contexts, where cohesion and centralized control often prevail, heterogeneous cultural orientations may introduce misalignment or increase decision-making complexity. At the same time, board size is an ambivalent variable. While it can broaden the skills and cognitive resources available for ESG risk management, in family contexts, it can also generate inefficiencies or slowdowns in the absence of formalized decision-making structures.

## 10.2 Future Research Directions

The literature review presented in the previous chapters has identified several thematic areas that warrant further development in future research. Below, we highlight the thematic areas and the related research questions that could be pursued.

### 10.2.1 Ownership Structures, Governance, and Risk Disclosure

The first area of research concerns the combined effect of hybrid ownership structures and unconventional governance structures on risk management. Non-family shareholders can enhance corporate risk-taking by diluting family control and introducing diverse perspectives. This is particularly evident when non-family shareholders actively participate in governance through ownership and board appointments, which can lead to a more balanced approach to risk-taking and long-term orientation in family firms (Du et al., 2022). Family businesses with multiple shareholder blocks could adopt innovative governance configurations such as ad hoc committees or family councils (Jungell, 2023). In such contexts, the balance between family control and managerial responsibility could influence both risk propensity and information transparency. The literature in our study shows that less traditional forms of control are often associated with tensions between family and managerial objectives, but also with new opportunities for strategic resilience. We therefore propose the following research question:

*RQ: How do hybrid ownership structures and unconventional boards interact in determining risk appetite and disclosure quality in family businesses?*

The biases of family members in charge influence the risk behavior of family businesses (Orlando et al., 2019). It would be interesting to analyze the impact of information asymmetries within the family. We therefore propose the following research question:

*RQ: How do intra-family information asymmetries influence disclosure quality and strategic risk decisions?*

Given that there is evidence that reputation-based voluntary disclosure reduces the cost of capital (Gantyowati et al., 2022), it would be interesting to investigate whether family businesses also use disclosure as a tool for legitimization toward external actors in contexts perceived as hostile or uncertain. We therefore propose the following research question:

*RQ: Do external perceptions of family reputation influence risk disclosure strategies and the cost of capital?*

### 10.2.2 Family Business Life Cycle, Succession, and Financial Structure

A second area of investigation focuses on generational transition and the firm's ability to absorb exogenous shocks. Generational transition is a time of vulnerability and identity renewal (Bergfeld & Bergfeld, 2023), which can influence risk tolerance and investment logic. Research on succession and risk in family businesses has primarily focused on managerial, asset, and leadership risks; however, very few studies address systemic external risks associated with succession. The new generation, often more sensitive to ESG issues, may assess the sustainability of the family business model differently and decide not to continue managing the business if they perceive that it is unable to adapt to these risks. We therefore propose the following research question:

*RQ: How do the younger generations' perceptions of climate and environmental risk affect their willingness to take on leadership roles in family businesses?*

The capital structure of family businesses reflects implicit values related to maintaining control (Gottardo & Moisello, 2019), as these businesses tend to favor debt over risk capital to avoid ownership dilution. Analyzing how these choices evolve over the life cycle of the business can help understand whether, and at what stages, these configurations are effective in mitigating the idiosyncratic risk associated with governance and generational transition. We therefore propose the following research question:

*RQ: Which financial structure configurations are most effective in mitigating idiosyncratic risk in the different stages of family business evolution?*

### 10.2.3 Innovation, Digitalization, and Strategic Risk

Innovation can be perceived as a threat to the stability of family wealth and control (De Massis et al., 2013). On the other hand, some family businesses adopt innovative strategies to ensure long-term continuity. In particular, incremental innovation, understood as a gradual improvement of processes, products, or services, seems to offer a middle ground between the need to adapt and the desire to preserve the family legacy (Calabrò et al., 2019). However, the literature has not yet investigated whether and how this form of innovation can be used strategically to mitigate the idiosyncratic risk associated with succession processes. Therefore, the following research question is proposed:

*RQ: How do family businesses use incremental innovation to mitigate the idiosyncratic risk associated with generational succession?*

Digitalization is perceived as either a threat or an opportunity, depending on the generation and the dominant family culture (Zapata-Cantu et al., 2023). Literature has focused on digitalization as a tool for growth or resilience. However, its impact on risk management in the context of family businesses needs to be explored (Madonna et al., 2025), as the introduction of AI and automation in decision-making processes raises unique questions for family businesses, where risk is often managed informally. We therefore propose the following research question:

*RQ: How does the adoption of AI-based digital technologies change risk perception and management in multi-generational family businesses?*

### 10.2.4 Internationalization and Risk

The literature on the internationalization of family businesses highlights a marked caution in foreign expansion processes, often attributed to their risk aversion and desire to preserve control and socioemotional assets (De Massis et al., 2018). However, the extent to which the perception of risk is associated with target countries' conditions, the timing and sequence of entry into foreign markets, remains largely unexplored. While some studies have highlighted the gradual nature of international strategies (Kontinen & Ojala, 2010), there is a lack of in-depth analysis of how country risk perception may directly influence the timing trajectories adopted by family businesses. We therefore propose the following research question:

*RQ: How does the perception of country risk influence the timing and gradualness of international entry in family businesses?*

The family brand, often linked to the founder's name, is an intangible asset that must be carefully protected. In this context, reputational risk assumes particular importance, especially during expansion processes into cultural contexts that are distant or perceived as dissonant with family values (Kano & Verbeke, 2018). Although the literature has explored the influence of cultural proximity on strategic adaptation (Kalhor, 2024), the question remains open as to whether and how cultural and linguistic similarity can serve as a lever to mitigate the reputational risk perceived by family businesses undergoing international expansion. We therefore propose the following research question:

*RQ: How do cultural and linguistic proximity mitigate the reputational risk perceived by family businesses during internationalization?*

### 10.2.5 CSR, ESG, and Reputational Risk Management

In family businesses, corporate social responsibility practices are often profoundly influenced by the family's value structure and internal culture. In addition to formal mechanisms such as ESG boards or committees, informal tools, including family councils, unregulated codes of ethics, and generational agreements, are increasingly important in defining the identity and credibility of ethical commitment (Hughes et al., 2025). However, the literature has focused mainly on the institutional and formal dimensions of CSR, neglecting the actual capacity of soft mechanisms to integrate or replace standard governance (Ghinizzini et al., 2025). We therefore suggest the following research question:

*RQ: To what extent do family councils, internal ethical codes, and generational pacts contribute to the credibility of CSR in family businesses, and can they act as alternative or complementary tools to formal governance in mitigating reputational risk?*

The adoption of ESG practices in family businesses has grown in response to regulatory, reputational, and stakeholder pressures. However, in many cases, implementation translates into symbolic practices with little to no real impact on business processes, resulting in greenwashing or tokenism (Zhu et al., 2025). This scenario raises questions about which ESG metrics help distinguish between genuine commitment and communication facades, and above all, which are most predictive of the reputational resilience of family businesses in times of crisis or transition. We therefore propose the following research question:

*RQ: Which ESG metrics are most predictive of reputational resilience in family businesses, and how do they distinguish between symbolic and substantive practices, given the risks of greenwashing and tokenism?*

Family narrative is a central element of identity for many family businesses, serving as a lever for long-term brand building and trust (Moisello, 2025). In international contexts, particularly in emerging markets, this narrative can interact in complex ways with corporate ESG strategies, generating implicit expectations among institutional investors. Although recent studies have analyzed the role of investors in promoting ESG transparency in family firms (Hughes et al., 2025), the narrative dimension remains largely unexplored. Understanding how and when family narratives contribute to investors' risk perception is crucial, especially in fluid cultural and regulatory contexts such as those of emerging markets. We therefore propose the following research question:

*RQ: How do family narratives and ESG strategies influence institutional investors' risk perception in family businesses operating in emerging markets?*

Finally, although our empirical analysis shows that board demographic diversity is not associated with reduced ESG controversies in family firms, the mechanisms underlying this relationship remain poorly understood. Quantitative data cannot reveal how diversity is experienced, interpreted, or negotiated within the specific cultural context of family governance. To uncover these dynamics, qualitative research methods such as case studies or interviews with board members and family stakeholders would be valuable for exploring the informal norms, trust dynamics, and communicative practices that mediate the impact of diversity on ESG oversight. Such methods can illuminate whether and how diversity becomes an asset or a liability in managing non-financial risk in family firms. We therefore propose the following research question:

*RQ: How do cultural and demographic differences within family firm boards interact with informal governance logics, and under what conditions do they support or constrain effective ESG risk management?*

# References


Allison, T. H., & Anglin, A. H. (2025). The power of family firm image in rewards-based crowdfunding. *Journal of Small Business Management*, 1–34.

Anderson, R. C., Duru, A., & Reeb, D. M. (2009). Founders, heirs, and corporate opacity in the United States. *Journal of Financial Economics, 92*(2), 205–222.

Arrondo-García, R., Fernández-Méndez, C., & Menéndez-Requejo, S. (2016). The growth and performance of family businesses during the global financial crisis: The role of the generation in control. *Journal of Family Business Strategy, 7*(4), 227–237.

Bergfeld, A. F., & Bergfeld, M. M. (2023). Next-generation entrepreneurial identity in family business systems: The influence of role-changing events on the understanding of legacy, individual identity, and transgenerational entrepreneurship of next-generation family business principals. *Thunderbird International Business Review, 65*(4), 399–408.

Berrone, P., Cruz, C., & Gomez-Mejia, L. R. (2012). Socioemotional wealth in family firms: Theoretical dimensions, assessment approaches, and agenda for future research. *Family Business Review, 25*(3), 258–279.

Bornhausen, A. M., & Wulf, T. (2024). Digital innovation in family firms: The roles of non-family managers and transgenerational control intentions. *Small Business Economics, 62*(4), 1429–1448.

Calabrò, A., Vecchiarini, M., Gast, J., Campopiano, G., De Massis, A., & Kraus, S. (2019). Innovation in family firms: A systematic literature review and guidance for future research. *International Journal of Management Reviews, 21*(3), 317–355.

Chalus-Sauvannet, M. C., Deschamps, B., & Cisneros, L. (2016). Unexpected succession: When children return to take over the family business. *Journal of Small Business Management, 54*(2), 714–731.

Craig, J. B., Pohjola, M., Kraus, S., & Jensen, S. H. (2014). Exploring relationships among proactiveness, risk-taking and innovation output in family and non-family firms. *Creativity and Innovation Management, 23*(2), 199–210.

De Massis, A., Frattini, F., & Lichtenthaler, U. (2013). Research on technological innovation in family firms: Present debates and future directions. *Family Business Review, 26*(1), 10–31.

De Massis, A., Frattini, F., Majocchi, A., & Piscitello, L. (2018). Family firms in the global economy: Toward a deeper understanding of internationalization determinants, processes, and outcomes. *Global Strategy Journal, 8*(1), 3–21.

Du, S., Ma, L., & Li, Z. (2022). Non-family shareholder governance and corporate risk-taking: Evidence from Chinese family-controlled businesses. *Journal of Business Research, 145*, 156–170.

Gantyowati, E., Rohman, A., Achmad, T., & Setiawan, D. (2022). reputation-based disclosure and cost of capital: The role of controlling ownership. *International Journal of Business & Society, 23*(1), 359–370.

García-Piqueres, G., Serrano-Bedia, A. M., & Pérez-Pérez, M. (2019). Knowledge management practices and innovation outcomes: The moderating role of risk-taking and proactiveness. *Administrative Sciences, 9*(4), 75.

George, G., Wiklund, J., & Zahra, S. A. (2005). Ownership and the internationalization of small firms. *Journal of Management, 31*(2), 210–233.

Ghinizzini, V., Benfante, C., Magri, C., & Gabrielli, G. (2025). Does the governance of Italian-listed family firms impact the reporting of social aspects? *Social Responsibility Journal, 21*(7), 1529–1548.

Giacomarra, M., Shams, S. R., Crescimanno, M., Sakka, G., Gregori, G. L., & Galati, A. (2021). Internal vs. external R&D teams: Evidences from the Italian wine industry. *Journal of Business Research, 128*, 752–761.

Gómez-Mejía, L. R., Haynes, K. T., Núñez-Nickel, M., Jacobson, K. J., & Moyano-Fuentes, J. (2007). Socioemotional wealth and business risks in family-controlled firms: Evidence from Spanish olive oil mills. *Administrative Science Quarterly, 52*(1), 106–137.

Gomez-Mejia, L. R., Makri, M., & Kintana, M. L. (2010). Diversification decisions in family-controlled firms. *Journal of Management Studies, 47*(2), 223–252.

Gottardo, P., & Moisello, A. M. (2019). *Capital structure, earnings management, and risk of financial distress: A comparative analysis of family and non-family firms*. Springer.

Hiebl, M. R., Duller, C., & Neubauer, H. (2019). Enterprise risk management in family firms: Evidence from Austria and Germany. *The Journal of Risk Finance, 20*(1), 39–58.

Hughes, M., Hu, Q., Simeonova, B., Ge, B., Issah, W. B., Jack, S., ... & Dai, S. (2025). ESG in family firms: A review of research, regulations and practice guidance.

Jian, J., He, K., Liu, Y., & Sun, Y. (2024). Corporate social responsibility: Opportunistic behavior under earnings management? *Asia-Pacific Journal of Accounting & Economics, 31*(2), 247–268.

Jungell, L. (2023). *Family governance: Managing dispersed ownership within the owning family through procedural justice*. Doctoral thesis, Hanken School of Economics, Helsinki.

Kalhor, E. (2024). Institutional effects on family business internationalization: A systematic review. *ZFW–Advances in Economic Geography, 68*(1), 41–62.

Kano, L., & Verbeke, A. (2018). Family firm internationalization: Heritage assets and the impact of bifurcation bias. *Global Strategy Journal, 8*(1), 158–183.

Kontinen, T., & Ojala, A. (2010). The internationalization of family businesses: A review of extant research. *Journal of Family Business Strategy, 1*(2), 97–107.

Le Breton-Miller, I., & Miller, D. (2009). Agency vs. stewardship in public family firms: A social embeddedness reconciliation. *Entrepreneurship Theory and Practice, 33*(6), 1169–1191.

Leppäaho, T., & Ritala, P. (2022). Surviving the coronavirus pandemic and beyond: Unlocking family firms' innovation potential across crises. *Journal of Family Business Strategy, 13*(1), 100440.

Llanos-Contreras, O., Arias, J., & Maquieira, C. (2021). Risk taking behavior in Chilean listed family firms: A socioemotional wealth approach. *International Entrepreneurship and Management Journal, 17*(1), 165–184.

Madonna, S., Cestari, G., & Georgiev, M. G. (2025). Unveiling risk management dynamics in family businesses through a bibliometric analysis. *Journal of Family Business Management*. https://doi.org/10.1108/JFBM-09-2024-0231

Memili, E., & Koç, B. (2023). The antecedents of family firms' resilience to crisis in hospitality and tourism. *International Journal of Hospitality Management, 113*, 103526.

Miller, D., Le Breton-Miller, I., & Lester, R. H. (2011). Family and lone founder ownership and strategic behaviour: Social context, identity, and institutional logics. *Journal of Management Studies, 48*(1), 1–25.

Moisello, A. M. (2025). From heritage to sustainability: A systematic literature review of family wineries. *Journal of Family Business Management*. https://doi.org/10.1108/JFBM-02-2025-0054

Orlando, B., Renzi, A., Sancetta, G., & Vagnani, G. (2019). Overconfidence and risk behavior in family firms. In *Corporate governance: Search for the advanced practices; Conferences Proceedings* (pp. 28–29). Virtus Interpress.

Özbay, D., Adıgüzel, H., & Karahan Gökmen, M. (2023). Corporate social responsibility and tax avoidance: Channeling effect of family firms. *Journal of Corporate Accounting & Finance, 34*(3), 11–30.

Roffia, P., Simón-Moya, V., & Sendra García, J. (2022). Board of director attributes: Effects on financial performance in SMEs. *International Entrepreneurship and Management Journal, 18*(3), 1141–1172.

Suchman, M. C. (1995). Managing legitimacy: Strategic and institutional approaches. *Academy of Management Review, 20*(3), 571–610.

Villagrasa, J., Escribá-Esteve, A., Donaldson, C., & Sánchez-Peinado, E. (2024). Firms financial strength during crisis periods: Does "familiness" matter? *Journal of Family Business Management*. https://doi.org/10.1108/jfbm-02-2024-0042

Wu, S. F., Fang, C. Y., & Chen, W. (2020). Corporate governance and stock price crash risk: Evidence from Taiwan. *Managerial and Decision Economics, 41*(7), 1312–1326.

Wu, S. W., Lin, F., & Wu, C. M. (2014). Corporate social responsibility and cost of capital: An empirical study of the Taiwan stock market. *Emerging Markets Finance and Trade, 50*(Suppl 1), 107–120.

Yang, M., Wang, Y., Bai, L., & Maresova, P. (2023). Corporate social responsibility, family involvement, and stock price crash risk. *Corporate Social Responsibility and Environmental Management, 30*(3), 1204–1225.

Zapata-Cantu, L., Sanguino, R., Barroso, A., & Nicola-Gavrilă, L. (2023). Family business adapting a new digital-based economy: Opportunities and challenges for future research. *Journal of the Knowledge Economy, 14*(1), 408–425.

Zellweger, T. M., & Nason, R. S. (2008). A stakeholder perspective on family firm performance. *Family Business Review, 21*(3), 203–216.

Zhu, F., Fan, H., & Zheng, Z. (2025). The disclosure fog: Institutional investors and corporate greenwashing. *International Journal of Finance & Economics., 30*, 3856–3874.

Zhu, Z., & Kang, Y. (2022). A far-reaching parental love? Co-governance of intergenerational succession and innovation activities in Chinese family firms. *Management and Organization Review, 18*(2), 358–394.

MIX
Papier aus verantwortungsvollen Quellen
Paper from responsible sources
FSC® C105338
FSC
www.fsc.org

If you have any concerns about our products,
you can contact us on
**ProductSafety@springernature.com**

In case Publisher is established outside the EU,
the EU authorized representative is:
**Springer Nature Customer Service Center GmbH**
**Europaplatz 3, 69115 Heidelberg, Germany**

Printed by Libri Plureos GmbH
in Hamburg, Germany